A MIRROR OF BEFORE AND AFTER

A MIRROR OF BEFORE AND AFTER

FRANK MOORE

Other books by Frank Moore:

Art of a Shaman

Chapped Lap

Cherotic Magic Revised

Deep Conversations In The Shaman's Den, Volume I

Frankly Speaking: A Collection of Essays, Writings and Rants

How to Handle an Anthropologist:
Russell Shuttleworth, PhD interviews shaman/performance artist Frank Moore

Skin Passion

The Cherotic (r)Evolutionary Complete 1991-1999

The Uncomfortable Zones of Fun: The Temescal Period 2009-2013

What A Life: An (auto)Biography of Shaman/Performance Artist Frank Moore

A Mirror of Before and After

Copyright 2025 by Inter-Relations

All rights reserved.

Inter-Relations
PO Box 1931
Eagle, ID 83616

Print ISBN: 978-1-7346850-7-7

Cover and book design by Michael LaBash.

For all the oddballs and misfits.

Moe, 1992

Table of Contents

Chapter I **1**
Chapter II **3**
Chapter III **5**
Chapter IV **7**
Chapter V **26**
Chapter V - Part 2 .... **31**

PART II THE SECOND VISIT

Chapter VI **33**
Chapter VII **36**
Chapter VIII **38**
Chapter IX **43**
Chapter X **45**
Chapter XI **48**
Chapter XII **54**
Chapter XIII **58**
Chapter XIV **62**
Chapter XV **66**
Chapter XVI **68**
Chapter XVII **70**
Chapter XVIII **75**
Chapter XIX **80**
Chapter XX **88**
Chapter XXI **92**
Chapter XXII.. .... **110**
Chapter XXIII **112**
Chapter XXIV.. .... **114**

Mirror of Before and After - a film proposal **125**

About Frank Moore **140**
Frank Moore Online **144**

Frank Moore, 1970

CHAPTER 1

People see themselves in me. They do not see the real me. Seeing themselves helps them to see their own beauty. Talking aloud to themselves in the form of another person helps them to grow.

For most of my life, there was a silk black screen between me and the world. I made noises. Even those who could decipher my code, could just spell from my noises a word or two -- a word or a sentence. I was a pure mirror upon which people could project any self-image, tell any secret without fear or inhibition. I was a mirror, a treasure box of secrets. When I got my unicorn horn, so I could type and spell out words on a letterboard, my role somewhat changed. But I still was a mirror and am still one.

Don't just stand there. Talk to me. My name is Unicorn. I talk by means of this board.

Yes, I am a mirror. You don't see me, the total me. In the illusion of seeing and talking to me, you are seeing a reflection of yourself.

I am a mirror without a frame, sitting outside the Student Center … in the Bus Stop Café … in the park … in the Mind Vendor Headshop … in Mother Lizard's Ball. Watching you buy your American flag bellbottoms. Watching. Watching you eat your cheeseburgers. Watching you smoke your dope and play with your soap bubbles. Watching you as you come in from hitching across country. I hear your secrets, your hopes, your plans, your dreams. But you rarely notice me watching and listening. I am so visible that I am invisible. A mirror without a frame. A spy from your spirit.

Sometimes you hear a laugh ... or maybe you smell the smell of unwashed armpits and unwiped ass, and you turn around. I am there. You see me, even when turned away and pretending not to see the slobbering idiot in the wheelchair. No, I am not an idiot. I am for you a symbol of death and insanity. You have made yourself believe that you aren't going to die, or even get seriously sick. You think you are in the Pepsi Generation and are going strong. You've got a lot to live, and Pepsi has a lot to give. But deep inside you, you know you are not only dying but are already dead. And Pepsi can't give you life. You've put a shell of fiction around your knowledge and are living in that fiction. But I poke holes in your fiction ... some of you run out screaming, "Exhibitionist," trying to patch up your fiction.

I am indeed an exhibitionist. I have a certain control over the mirror image ... not always ... and never the complete control ... sometimes I become trapped in the mirror. A mirror doesn't have its own identity: it is what it reflects. But I wanted an identity. I wanted to find me, to be me. I wanted people, especially chicks, to see me as me, not as a reflection, like me ... and yes, even to love me for what I, who I, really was. So for most of my life I fought against the mirror role.

But I always got suckered into it in my desire to show people their own beauty, suckered into it by my emotions; and the role trapped me again. But somewhere along the line I accepted the role, wanted to go into it fully.

CHAPTER II

The Before and After was the peak of materiality. Dudes, chicks, fags, blacks, whores. Kids seven years old ditching school and hanging around in the store, smoking on the car seats under the candle shelf. A little black kid trying to decide whether to put the cigarette or his thumb into his mouth. Junior high girls meeting and teasing the boys. The older hangers-on eyeing the fresh ripe melons on jail-bait chicks. Teenage boys trying to catch a glimpse of a brown tit as chicks tried see-through shirts on behind a curtain. Spades trying to be cool. Rock musicians trying to be hip. Fat middle-aged mommas and poppas trying to recapture Youth, to be where it's at. Secretaries, nurses, college co-eds, buying bait to catch breadwinners. Dudes hanging out … waiting to be accepted by the merchant marines' school … waiting for the next key to come through the store … or just waiting for something to wait for. Zap Comics with Captain Pissgums and Honeybunch, hash pipes, spoons, American flag fringe jackets, blacklights, leather pants, posters, smile but John Lennon kept singing, "God is a concept by which we measure our pain," over and over again on the robot record player as we, too lazy to run up a tower to change the record, said "Right on!"

We too believed only in ourselves … at least the Before and After crew thought they did. Smoking dope in the back room, three o'clock in the morning after closing the store, after selling the last lid to the last longhair, Thai, exchange student in a gray trench coat. All except Moe, my big, bush-haired friend who ran the shop.

Moe didn't do dope, drink, smoke; he really believed in himself. HE DIDN'T NEED TO GET HIGH BECAUSE HE WAS ALREADY THERE. He was the undercurrent of love, real love, in the store. He sold the fancy leather bags, sash pouches, and belts smelling of the ether of the independent hip artisans for no profit. Moe was a strong man that could do anything because he believed in himself and didn't give a shit about anything. But that was an illusion, and I saw through it.

Why couldn't I stop seeing through the surface into the other things? Moe was trapped in a prison called Before and After, the curse that his chrome-plated society Jewish mother had zapped upon him, the cross that he foolishly carried to ease his father's loneliness. Now he said he controlled his own life.

He didn't control even the heat in the store. He sat there, stripped to his waist, waiting, sweating in the heat that some asshole miles away decided to give to the store. Waiting, with coconut incense and perfumed candles to hide the body odor … trapped in the store without a shower … sneaking out once every two weeks in P-coat and multi-colored sunglasses. Sitting, waiting with his spears of irony, keeping people from getting too close to the real Moe. Pretending to be satisfied sleeping with chicks with bib tits on the back-room floor. Pretending to be happy, to be doing his thing, when all the while he really wanted to ride the chopper that sat in the middle of the storeroom, to ride with his furry buffalo horns, searching for that Something. But now pretending everything.

On acid one time, I saw Moe as he would become … an old Jewish storekeeper, imprisoned behind a tired, sad face. Talking to the dudes who hang around. Talking about how it was on the merchant marine's ship. How the men made one another look like queers. Jimmy Hendrix was on the record player playing Foxy Lady. Philip, a skinny doper, described how Hendrix had jerked off his guitar at Woodstock. Quite a showman, that motherfucker.

CHAPTER III

I wanted to scream. Moe, why are you doing this to yourself? How did you get yourself into this mess? Get out of this ... Get out of here! Beat it! Run like the clothes you sell are filled with heroin and all of your "friends" are undercover narcs, run like the cops are coming to arrest you! Run! Ride out of here on your bike. That is why I came here ... to take you back. But you have gotten yourself into this mess, into this store with clothes and hollow giant candles filled with millions of dollars of smack. But you wouldn't come, you stubborn motherfucker! Why wouldn't you? But now it's too late. You've got to leave right now, leaving me here in the store to face the pigs, the male nurses in white who like to hit people, and the rest of their monster crew. I am no backstage cowboy. I will maintain. I will give you time to get out of the city. But go now!

I always have wondered what the cops would do if they caught me. Well, this will blow their minds: a cripple on a ton of dope. I will piss when they lift me into the squad car. I will outsmart them. Better yet, safer too, I'll play crazy, the idiot. They will never know that I'm on acid. Okay, give me the water. It'll be a long time before they will give me any. But then go. Why won't you go?

That was the one trip when I was glad that I couldn't move about because I wanted to kick the balls of every pimple-faced, greasy-haired "informer" and "bully cop" who turned out to be just buyers of hash pipes.

But the love between Moe and me was real. The store, even without the imagined heroin, which now seems absurd, was really a prison for Moe. Moreover, I was powerless to release Moe because he was unwilling to release himself.

CHAPTER IV

Suzy appeared during my first D.C. visit; she was lonely, caught in this world. But she couldn't be of this world. She would shatter if she had to stay here much longer.

It was hard to believe she was really real. Really a flesh and blood person. More like a sad spirit with pale, oval face with large, black eyes which went back for ages upon ages. I fell into them with I first saw her sitting on the tower step, just listening, just watching from somewhere far inside herself. Her hair was the only part of her that was happy. Long sunbeams, now red, now yellow. The sun of her hair surrounded the moon of her face. Pale, white milk with streaks of blue. Her hands were like a child's, with long, fragile fingers. Her body was so fragile, I was afraid she would blow away, vanish into the nothingness where she had come from. She just sat there on the step, bundled up in an old navy coat, looking sadly at me.

"What is your name?" I pointed out on my board. I knew she read it and understood it. She was not ignoring me. She wanted to answer me, but the words would not come out. Her lips moved a little, trying to form words. But she remained mute. Just sitting there looking sadly sad.

"Can you talk?" I asked.

She shook her head gravely no.

"If you want to talk, you could use my board," I said.

She thought about that for a while, and finally started spelling out words … her finger hovering over the unfamiliar board, trying to find letters. She could talk … that is, there wasn't anything physical stopping her voice from talking. She just forgot how to talk recently. Sometimes she could get a word or two out. But never around me during the two weeks there. She told me, however, that I was the first person she had talked more than three words to in a long time. She didn't smile either … for the simple reason that she didn't have anything to smile about. What reason could there be in a world that shatters you?

The first time, we started holding hands. But it was like holding hands with a China doll because every time I squeezed the slightest bit, she would let out a silent Ouch! I felt a strong tie between us. When I told her I loved her, a timid smile appeared for a moment and was gone again. It was an effort for the smile to push up through the sad mask. Suzy was up and out the door as if she was searching for the smile. She didn't come back for the next few days, and I almost forgot about her … almost, but not quite. Then about an hour from closing time, Suzy came tiredly in and, sitting down beside me, held my hand. For a long time, she just looked at me. She could have been a vampire … or an angel in some of the Italian paintings … or the mermaid who traded her fins for feet and had to walk on broken glass the rest of her life.

"What do you do?" I finally asked.

"Sometimes I sell underground papers … sometimes I sell pirated records. Maybe I could give you a Beatles or a Dylan record the next time I get some. Sometimes I take grass to different places for someone," Suzy spelled out.

"How?" I asked.

"I hitch," she said. But Suzy wouldn't tell me anything else about her activities. I envisioned a fat member of the Mafia giving little Suzy a brick of grass in a shoebox. Suzy walks slowly to the parkway and puts her thumb out, the shoebox under her arm. A big diesel truck stops to pick her up. Having a little trouble not dropping the box, she scrambles up into the cab and hands the greasy driver a note with a cigar which says, "I can't talk. I am going to Annapolis."

"Isn't that dangerous?" I asked.

"I don't know," she said, "I must rest now. I'll lie here a while … then I must go."

She lay down on the car seat beside my chair. She pulled my hand to hold it and fell asleep. As I sat there, listening to the music, looking down at her … she changed from a woman to a child to a small, sleeping animal back to a woman … I felt like I had someone; and yet, still felt alone. I wanted to make love to her. But I didn't want to freak her anymore than she already was. That was just a part of the reason. I didn't know how to ask a girl or how to let it happen. She looked so helpless. I wanted to help her and the only way to help her was for me to be a mirror and keep the channel open. If I asked her to make love to me, the mirror might break, and she might close off to me like she had to the world. That night I wouldn't risk it. Moe started to close shop. Suzy was still sleeping when it was time to lock up. Moe looked at her for a while.

"Does she want to stay here tonight?" he asked me in a hushed tone, but I didn't know. "Well, it looks like it would take an atom bomb to wake her. She looks too comfortable to move."

But as soon as he said that she sat straight up, her eyes wide with fear. It seemed that for a minute she didn't know where she was. After she adjusted, she motioned to an invisible wristwatch, wanting to know what time it was.

"It's three in the morning, time for all good girls to be in bed … bad girls, too," Moe said.

When she heard the time, Suzy was in a panic as if she had just missed a date. She tried to scoop up her things to run out of the store. But her hands just fumbled … and when she finally got her things together and stood up, she walked like she was drunk or dizzy. I didn't like this at all. Moe didn't either. He walked up behind her, picked her up and carried her back and sat down on the car seat with her on his lap.

"Now, let's talk this over like sensible people," Moe told Suzy. "It's three a.m. and it's freezing outside. In other words, it's not fit for taking a walk. And from the looks of you, you aren't fit for walking. So, you have two choices. You can stay here and sleep on the car seats while we sleep in the back room to protect your virtues. Or I'll drive you where you want to go … gentleman that I am. Which will it be? Will you keep us company?"

Suzy shook her head and just looked toward the door.

"O.K." said Moe, and added to me, "Hold down the fort. I'll lock the door behind me."

Moe carried Suzy as he would have carried me and banged the door shut. The record player was still going. "See me! Feel me! Touch me! Heal me!" Moe came back in twenty minutes and woke me up as he unlocked the door.

"A strange chick. She made me let her out at a corner on Pennsylvania and just waited until I drove away to move. It was like she didn't want me to know where she lives … if she lives anywhere, which I have my doubts," Moe said.

For a couple of days she didn't come back. I thought about her a lot … wondering if she had gotten in trouble on one of her trips … wondering how she survived in the city being so frail … wondering about her past. I knew nothing really about her except that her name was Suzy and she was lost in her mind. I kept waiting for her to come back, half expecting to see her every time I looked up from the Mr. Natural comic I was pretending to be reading ... and went back to the comic disappointed. Moe felt my disappointment and kept muttering, "You sure can pick 'em." When I asked him what he thought was the matter with Suzy and how I could help her, he just said, "I'm not saying anything is the matter with her. She is just into her own thing ... which I must admit is different." But Moe wouldn't give me any advice. To other people, he gave tons of wisdom coated in wisecracks. But I couldn't get any use out of his B.A. in psychology. He would just say, "I ain't your mother." One night, Suzy came in and laid down on the car seats to rest as before. After a little while, she sat up to talk to me.

"Would you believe me if I told you something?" she asked on the board.

"Try me."

"I hear voices inside of me. They tell me things to do and where to go."

"That is nothing unusual ... there is a voice inside of me too," I said. I knew what she was talking about and what I was talking about were two different things. But right then, that didn't make any difference. I wanted to get inside of her private world to guide her into our everyday world ... that is if her world wasn't better than ours.

"Do other people hear vices too?" she asked.

"Kind of."

"Then you don't think I am crazy?"

"Yes, you are quite crazy. But I am crazy too ... and proud of it."

"I talked to Jesus yesterday."

"Inside of yourself?"

"No. I had to walk a long way. I can't remember where I went or what street the room was on, so I can't go back again. But I will know where to go to meet Jesus the next time. I always know."

"Now?" I asked. The creeps were inside me, bordering on fear, but I hoped I acted like we were carrying on a normal conversation … not for the black couple who were standing nearby looking at bellbottoms. They couldn't hear us because we were talking through the board in another world. But I had to talk naturally about unnatural things for Suzy, to give her the freedom to talk. I didn't want to shut her up just because inside I felt creepy. "How do you know where to go?"

"The Voices. It was in a white room. Jesus said it is very important now for me to listen to the voices and do what they say. I was going to where he is soon if I'm in the right place when the time comes. The voices will guide me to the place, and then I will shatter."

There was no mistaking the word shatter. "Please don't shatter," I said.

"But I want to shatter and go back to the world I come from. I got nothing here."

"You have me. I love you."

"How can you love me?" Suzy asked, her eyes open wide. "I am not real. You can't love something that is not real, can you?"

"You are real. I can see you and touch you … that proves you are real …."

I stopped because there was a ball of sadness growing within me. She could have poked holes in everything I said. On acid, I had seen and touched things that weren't really there. If I was mistaken then, why couldn't I be seeing things now? She did look like a ghost. I thought these things while I was pointing out the words. I wasn't doubting my own sanity … or her realness. But if she started trying to argue, I wasn't sure that I could make her see that, while there are many realities, you got to be in the reality that you find yourself in and live like it is the only thing going. I wished I was like Moe who believed that this flesh and blood world was all there is ... there ain't no more ... you better grab it while you can. It would have been easier to pull Suzy into this world if I was like Moe. Why couldn't I be? I was sweating like a doctor delivering a baby, hoping it wouldn't be a still birth. I couldn't talk anymore because of the ball inside of me. I just sat there, looking at her.

"What is wrong?" Suzy asked, looking puzzled. "Why are you sad?"

"I need you here and you are going. Please don't go. Don't shatter. Try this world a couple of months more ... for me."

"I can't promise anything. I might shatter at any second. There is so much pain here. But I want to be with you. I have to go when the voices tell me. But I will come here when I can."

"And if you feel like shattering, come here to talk to me. Promise?"

"I can't promise. I think I can ... but I can't promise."

"I wish I could stay here in D.C. longer," I said.

"Aren't you staying here?" Suzy looked a little surprised and a little frightened.

"I'm just visiting over the vacation. I go to college in California and got to go back next Sunday to go back to school. You would like it out there ... it's warm and sunny. I have an apartment with my brother ..."

"I wish you could stay," Suzy said.

After that, Suzy started sleeping overnight on the car seats when she came to the store. I soon learned that she didn't have any concept of time, except when the voices told her to be at a place at an exact time. She didn't come back for three days after her last visit. But she thought she had been in only yesterday. She couldn't remember what she did during the three days. She just walked after she had left to a room where she had slept. When she woke up, she came right back to the shop. So I must be mistaken. Each time she came, Suzy was more open and happier ... not happy ... but the smile stayed on longer.

"Would you make love with me?" I had to ask the question one night. My link with her was stronger and I was more willing to take the risk.

"I don't think I can," she said, turning whiter ... whiter than usual. "I never did it before. Have you?"

"No."

"I don't know how to do it. I couldn't stand the terrible pain. I'd shatter in pieces under the pain. Someone ... I don't remember who ... told me about the pain making love is."

"I wouldn't hurt you. do you believe that?" I asked.

"Yes."

"Really, I don't know very much about sex," I said. I just knew what I had read, seen in movies and in dirty pictures. I knew as much as the normal virgin who took sex education, talked to his mother (but not to his father) freely, went to a few college parties, and lived with Moe, who wasn't a prude. I knew everything about sex, but really knew nothing about it ... nothing about making love, I didn't know even if I could make love. I thought that I must be able to since I could jack off. But I wasn't sure. But not being sure, wanting to find out, wasn't the reason why I felt pushed to make love, pushed hard by a red-hot branding iron. I know that I'd still be a man even if I couldn't make love. But I was tired of being a lonely mirror. A lonely mirror can't reflect clearly and truly. The loneliness coats the mirror and colors the reflection which could mislead or even kill the person who is looking into the mirror. The mirror was tired of people kissing their own images on its surface … not tired … the mirror wanted them to kiss their images, and finally love themselves. That was my purpose … to make them love themselves. But I wanted, needed, someone to kiss my face. That someone, a woman, would have to really see my face and love me before she could kiss me. I had never been really kissed in my life. I got henpecks, loud dramatic kinds and the kisses that you give your grandmother. But never a warm, real kiss. So I was a clouded mirror when I was around girls who I had fallen in love with in my head. That cloud kept me from just reflecting truly the images I loved most. I had to hold myself from exploding, breaking the image into dangerous pieces, cutting the beautiful face. I was trapped in my role, trying to do something with a clouded surface, and at the same time, trying to make myself seen by the girl … wishing for some way out … until it became so confusing that I had to leave and not come around again. I used to cry when this happened … one time for three days straight. And then I would go out again and play the mirror game … exposing myself and waiting for someone who could see me. There wasn't time for bitterness.

"It really is important for you to make love, isn't it?" Suzy asked. "Give me time … I am so afraid. Please don't be sad. I do want to make you happy … maybe I can learn how to make love. Give me time."

It wasn't worth it, having Suzy fret over what she couldn't do. I was beginning to see that she really could not make love, at least while she was in her own world. She would if she could; I knew, felt it. She would if there was time, because she was slowly opening up. But there was no time. I was leaving in less than a week. So I put my wantings away and tried to get her to tell me about her world. But the cloud was still there.

She opened more and more, brightening more each day she came to the store. Moe saw what was happening to her and kept saying, "When are you getting married?" Finally, the night came when tomorrow I had to fly to California.

"Why do you have to go away?" Suzy asked, looking sadly up at me.

"You know. I don't want to leave … but I have to."

"Why can't you stay? This is why I don't like your world. People are always going away just when I am getting warm. It hurts."

"I wish there was a way that I could take you there."

"I could hitch," Suzy said, then thought about it, looking into the air. "If I was free to go, I would hitch."

"Aren't you free to go if you want?"

"No."

"Why not?"

"The Past … a Curse." Her saying this left me in chills. "Please don't ask me questions."

"But if you want to come, then you should be free to come … there is always a way. But I don't like the idea of you hitching cross country. It's dangerous."

"But I hitch all the time," Suzy said, surprised at my worrying. I could just see Suzy being raped by some bull-chested Southern redneck in a beat-up old Dodge behind some run-down gas station. I didn't want to take the risk if we didn't have to. but I always took risks when I was by myself … for myself. So why was I so afraid of letting Suzy take risks?

"If you want to come to California … I suppose hitching is all right. I would worry about you, until you showed up. But that is my problem. If you really want to, then do it. It's OK if you don't want to."

"I want to, but I can't," Suzy said, asking for understanding with her eyes.

"Why?"

"I've already told you. I am under a curse. I cannot leave of my own free will."

"What kind of curse?"

She just stared blankly into space. I was beginning to feel like I was in a horror movie. Why couldn't it just be simple, without all these … things … what were they? … supernatural … creepy things being thrown at me?

"Why don't you trust me?" I asked, jabbing my pointer at the letters.

"I trust you," Suzy said, slowly moving her childlike finger over the board.

"No you don't! If you did, you would let me in on your secrets."

"How can I tell you when I don't know what the curse is? I only know that I am under it and trapped here."

"You are the only one who can break the curse by doing what you want to do … what you want … not what you are told by some voice. The voice is inside of you, but it isn't really you. Listen to yourself, your real self."

"But I am not real. I don't exist."

"Cut that out! You are feeling so you are real."

"But I can't feel anything. I can't because I don't exist." Tears were running silently down her face.

"If you don't feel, why are you crying?"

"Because I hurt. All I can feel in this world is pain. I want to shatter. Right now!"

"Why do you hurt?"

"Because I am hurting you … making you sad. I don't want you to be sad. But I can't help it."

"Do you love me?"

"Yes … I think so. But that's impossible because I don't exist. I can't love …. Why does that make you sad?"

"Because I love you and I don't …" I was lost in words again. Lost in the ball of sadness inside of me again. I felt like hitting that cameo face to prove to her her realness. I wished I could shake her so hard that the shell would break. She just sat there, not feeling her own tears, wondering why I felt sad … wondering what she had done. I had to calm down.

"If you don't really exist … I know you do exist, but what I know doesn't matter right now … reality doesn't matter. You don't exist. You love me and want to go to California with me … or at any case, you think so. But you don't exist, so you can't want anything or love anyone … Now, am I real?"

"You are the realest person I have met in this world."

"Since you are not real, nothing can matter to you. but I am real, and things do matter to me. Little things, like knowing you are OK. I want you to come out. You can stay at my apartment as long as you want. Or you can roam the streets if you want … at least, it is warm there."

"I want to … I would … but the curse."

"Why don't you just trust me? I studied magic … the real magic. There is no curse, no spell, that can trap a person who truly believes in himself. Also, one person can release another from under a spell if he believes in himself and if the enchanted person believes strongly enough in his friend. If you believe in me enough to come, then the curse will be broken. Believe in me. Do that much for me."

I didn't know where that came from. It was just one of those things that popped into my head. At times when I had just thrown what I thought was my last punch, the punch that didn't quite do the job, one of these things would come to me and I would follow it blindly, no matter how weird it sounded. This magic thing sounded freaky. But it had a true ring. And I could see that it struck Suzy. "Will you trust me that much?"

"I will hitch as soon as I can."

Moe came over, his bare chest sweating in the heat. "What are you two loons jabbering about?" he asked.

"Suzy is hitching to San Bernardino," I said.

"What for?" For this mutation?" Moe waved his head towards me. "You have shit for brains! But that isn't any of my business. Why not fly with him instead of hitching?"

For a long time, Suzy just sat there, trying to decide if she could talk to Moe through the board. She never talked to him before, except through hand motions. She finally pointed out. "How? I haven't any money."

"I'd be stupid not to notice. I'll make a package deal ... Tell you what I'm going to do, my little chickens. I'll sent you both on the jet tomorrow."

"Cut that out …. You're in the red now. You even tricked me into paying my way out here. If I had known how broke you were then, I wouldn't have come here in the first place. I feel like I am sponging off of you. Just see if I come here again until I can pay my way," I said.

"Oh, dry up, prune face! Who said I was broke? Have you seen my books? The fact is that I have five months back wages that I haven't collected. Bet you didn't know I had two silent partners who agreed before we opened the store to pay me $200 a month. I just put the money right back into the store. But legally, I would have a thousand even if the store sinks right now, which it won't. So, it is no skin off my back to send you two lovenicks back to where you belong." Moe ran out of breath, but caught it and went on raving, "But even if I were bankrupt, I have the right to give my last dollar to you if I want to without having to listen to your feeling guilty, asshole. If it would ease your small mind, you can pay me back with ten dollars a month."

"I'll do that," I said.

"I'm sure you will," Moe laughed ironically, but with a certain respect somewhere down deep. "Sexy Suzy, are you up for flying?"

"I could never fly. I am afraid of airplanes and heights," Suzy said.

"I don't blame you ... airplanes look too big to go up in the air. But they do stay up in the air ... most of the time. Flying is almost as much fun as ..."

"But I am still afraid," Suzy said.

"If you let fear run your life ... let it keep you from going where you want and doing what you want ... you are not free. Fear is only in your head, and you are the master of your won head ... well, ain't you" Moe could have been a preacher, a rabbi, if he believed in God.

Suzy just sat there in silence.

"Do you want to do?" Moe asked.

"Yes," Suzy said.

"Is there anyone who would keep you here?"

"No. I have no one."

"Then you are flying?"

"Maybe," Suzy said. For the first time, I felt a note of mischief in her, something that was always hidden by her sadness and gloom. Although I didn't like the maybe answer, this new feeling told me that the mirror was getting results.

Moe walked from us towards the back room saying, "If you two ever make up your minds, you know where to find me."

"Does he really mean it … about paying my way? Can he afford it?" Suzy asked me.

"If you knew him better, you wouldn't ask such sane questions. Of course he meant it … and of course, he can't afford it. but if you don't take him up on it, he will be insulted. You'd be lucky to get him to call you shithead months afterwards. But I'll pay him back even if I have to trick him into taking my checks."

"Do you have to go tomorrow? Couldn't you wait for a few more days?"

"My first class is Monday morning, the day after tomorrow. So, I have to go."

"Do you believe that I want to go with you? I'll even fly with you." Suzy shivered at the thought of flying, licked her lips nervously, and went on, "I will fly with you if you wait for a few days."

"I do know that you want to go. But how long do you want me to wait?"

"I don't know … it depends on how long it takes to do what I have to do. But you can't wait. You have things to do too. I'll hitch when I have done the things. Sometime … maybe."

"I hate it when you answer 'maybe' and 'sometime'. Those two words don't exist, neither do 'fear' and 'can't'. They don't exist in the language. Are you coming … yes, or no?"

"Maybe," Suzy said stubbornly, sad that she couldn't say anything else. She thought for a long while, then said, "I will come soon. Soon."

"Promise?"

"I can't promise. But I will come soon." Suzy thought for a minute, and then asked, "If I tell you something, you won't tell anyone?"

"No."

"Promise?"

"I promise … I can promise things because I know I can do what I want," I said.

"I escaped from a mental hospital in New York a year ago. I ran away from home when I was seventeen after my parents tried to kill me. They tried many times to do it. So, I ran away. We lived in the country in West Virginia. I just walked away. I got to New York, but the police picked me up. I couldn't talk then either, and I didn't have any I.D. They couldn't find out who I was or where I came from. So, they called me Suzy and put me into the hospital."

"What is your real name?"

"I can't remember. It isn't important, is it?"

"Not to me. But you should have some I.D. so when the cops stop you, they won't bother you … unless you are carrying grass."

"They never pick me up," Suzy said, "They can't catch me again. Never again."

"But you were caught that first time, weren't you?" I asked.

"Yes. But I escaped from the hospital after a year and came here. Since then, I have been protected by the voices. So, if I don't disobey the voices, the policemen can't catch me. That is why I can't fly with you tomorrow. There is one more thing I have to do … people are depending on me. I can't let them down."

"What do you have to do?" I asked, thinking it was likely to be some kind of dope deal in which she was letting herself be used as the go-between. She had guts to live like she did … no, it was foolishness, which was almost like having guts except it was mixed with fear. A deadly combination.

"One of my friends is in a mental hospital near Baltimore. I have to go tomorrow and stay overnight to help him escape."

"How?" I felt like I was asking a calm, but mad, scientist how he was going to blow up the world.

"the same way I did. Walk out."

"Simple."

"Yes. But he needs me to do it."

"I need you too … free and safe. If you do it, they will put you in there, too."

"They can't do that, because I am protected … Why won't you believe that?" Suzy asked, wondering why I couldn't accept simple facts.

"Come to California instead."

She looked shocked, disappointed at me, "Leave him there? Don't ask me not to do what I have to do."

It wasn't any good trying to argue logically with her, telling her the reasons why her mission was impossible and why it was dangerous. The reasons just didn't exist in her world. Why was she afraid of everything except what was the most dangerous? The thought ran through my mind that she was just making the whole thing up as an excuse not to fly with me. But it was too far out to be an excuse. Suzy would just walk into the hospital without a plan, a plot, in her head, and walk out with her friend. It was so insane that it might have worked. It was her life and I wan't her mother; but the risks that she was taking gave me a clammy feeling. I made her write down Moe's name and the store's phone number to put in her little handbag … just in case.

"Stop worrying about me." Suzy gave a little laugh … a silent giggle. Did she really laugh? A warm feeling spread over inside of my body, replacing the cold dread. She really laughed … it wasn't my imagination. It was a pin prick laugh that most people wouldn't have noticed. Suzy had not been smiling two weeks before. I don't know why she laughed … maybe because of how funny I look worrying so much. But the laugh released me from worry, letting me go home with something even if Suzy might never come. I still wanted her to come and would be sad if she didn't come. But the feeling that we were in right then was all that mattered … for right then.

"I will come after I help my friend," Suzy said.

When we told this to Moe, he just said, "I'll ship her C.O.D. in a week to you."

Suzy stayed that night after we had a party, eating the carry-out eggrolls and some chicken shit from the Peking Restaurant next door. Suzy was sitting on the chair … cross-legged, rocking back and forth as she ate with her fingers. Smiling. Happy. I wished that this was the last picture I had of her. But the next morning she stood in the rain, watching Moe put me into the car. Moe tried to push her in after me, but she had to do her mission. She just stood there, crying in the rain. This is the last time that I will see her. She will never come out. She will stay under the Curse, getting caught or trapped. She was still standing there, staring after us, as we made the U-turn and headed for the airport. This is the last time I will see her.

CHAPTER V

I hassled with the airlines for two days, and finally arrived in L.A. My nineteen-year-old brother, Jerry, was waiting for me. When we got out of the parking lot I told him about Suzy. "A girl is coming out to live with me. She would have flown with me today if she hadn't had something to clear up first. She will probably fly out in a week."

"Well, what about our living situation?" Jerry grumbled, playing with his black hair, grown long since he got away from Dad and into the apartment five months ago. "I guess I'm supposed to drive here and pick her up?"

"Yes." I wasn't expecting this kind of attitude from Jerry. I thought he would share in my joy. He knew how long I had waited to have a girlfriend and how badly I had wanted on.

"Where will she sleep ... with you?" Jerry asked.

"It isn't that kind of thing ... yet. She can sleep on the hide-away."

"You have everything planned out, haven't you? Does she have any money to help with the rent and buy food?"

"No."

"Nice. So, we support her. Nice!"

This pissed me off. We had been supporting Jerry's girl, Lynn, for months. In fact, that was why he took the job of taking care of me

… so Dad wouldn't blow a fuse finding the two lovers sleeping together in his castle. Lynn was supposed to be living in the university dorm, but spent most nights at our place, eating our food, which Jerry cooked. Somehow, I got switched from my double bed in the bedroom to the single bed in the front room to give the lovers privacy and room. And I spent a great deal of time just sitting, waiting … my hat fallen off … having to piss … waiting for Jerry to come back … he'd say he'd just be an hour, visiting Lynn at the dorm or driving her somewhere and it would be four hours. I let go of all that. It didn't really piss me off at all. Jerry, if immature and a little unreliable, was a good kid and brother. He had his life to live, and I wasn't about to hold him back. But why couldn't I expect the same thing from him? I had my own life to live, too. That was what pissed me off … hurt me.

I came home with something to share, something new in my life and Jerry didn't see how important it was to me. Well, if Suzy came out, he would have to accept her because he needed me as much as I needed him. He needed the $250 welfare paid him to live with me. He needed the freedom that our apartment gave him. He didn't want to move back to Mom and Dad's or get a "real" job, as Dad would say. So, if Suzy came, he would have to accept her. If she came … I quickly covered up that thought. She was coming.

After three hot, smoggy, overcrowded hours on the freeway, we finally got home, and I finally took the piss I'd been waiting for and drink a quart of water … the place was a mess; Mom hadn't gone shopping for us that week. But it didn't matter because we were just dropping by our apartment to get Jerry's drums and soon split to Mom's. Jerry had band practice and Dad wanted to inspect our green station wagon for dents … for excuses to threaten to pull His underaged son back under His roof and to take the car away.

It was our ritual to go over, for Dad to blow up and get ready to take the car back into his garage, for Mom to attack him arguing that without the car, Jerry couldn't drive me to college, and we would have to move back home. I tried to stay out of it, eating the good food and sitting in the reclining chair watching the color TV. But it was hard to stay out of an absurd thing. As much as I like Mom's cooking, I would prefer to eat the greasy Col. Sanders' fried chicken and live in litter until Jerry learned that freedom means that Mother isn't there picking up after him and cooking his food. By helping us, Mom was really undermining us. I saw this and kept telling them about it. but I was too weak to do anything. Mom was a magnet that was pulling me backward to her, keeping me in her force field. Jerry pretended that he was free. I knew I wasn't free, but I wanted to be and was willing to do anything to set myself free. When Jerry told her about my unknown girl who I thought was coming to live with us, Mom said, "You have to be realistic. Do you really think she will come?"

"She said she would."

"Like Betty said she would go out on a date with you, and then called me asking how she could get out of it without hurting your feelings. She was afraid of encouraging you because you might get too serious."

"All I asked her to do was to go to a party with me ... not sleep with me or marry me. Besides, this is different. Suzy is coming out to live with me. I don't know what will develop from there."

"Can she take care of you? Should Jerry start looking for another job?" Mom asked, as Jerry started fidgeting on the green sofa. "You should think of these facts of life."

"Suzy is too weak to take care of me. I still need Jerry ... he won't lose his job," I said. "I can't understand this. You know how I have wanted this ... for how long. You said you wanted this for me. But now when it looks like it might happen ... I don't know if it will happen ... it might fall through ... but it looks like it might happen. Now, you are not with me. You keep throwing all these things at me, making me feel a little bit guilty about having her come out."

"You should have some consideration for me. It is my place too," Jerry said.

"I do have consideration for you. I don't do dope there. My friends don't come around much because they make you uneasy. I understand all of that and it's okay. But this is important. I can't understand why we are talking about it."

"I just don't want you to get hurt," Mom said. "Why can't you settle for some handicapped girl? Why must you keep pushing into something that always gets you hurt?"

"If a handicapped girl attracts me, I'll ... not settle for her ... just try to get close to her just like I try to with any girl who attracts me. But I am not going to feel guilty because no girl in a wheelchair has turned me on ... not because of the wheelchair, but I haven't found one who has the same interests ... who wanted to live in the world."

"Stop being a snob. Lower your standards. Why do you always go for the pretty girls with whom you don't have a chance. How many times of being crushed before you stop letting yourself be hurt?" Mom asked.

"As long as it takes. I can't stop just because I got hurt before. Maybe the next time it will be different. But if I didn't take risks and go after what I wanted, it would pass ... and I would never know. I'd rather get hurt than not know."

After a long pause, Mom asked, "What's the matter with her?"

"What makes you think that anything is the matter with her?" I asked.

"Because any girl that would want you must be sick."

I simply started bawling. What else could I do? I just cried. I couldn't stop crying.

How could she say that? How could she believe it? I would have expected Dad to say that; it wouldn't have touched me if he was the one speaking. He never did understand me, even though he loved me. It wouldn't have bothered me.

But I was helpless, defenseless, when Mom's belief in me turned out to be not there at all. I told her everything … almost everything … over the dinner table each day when she was feeding me … talking about philosophy and religion … telling her about my first acid trip so she could write her term paper on drugs. She pushed me into things when I was a kid, treating me like a normal kid. Cut Scouts, Boy Scouts, Sunday School. Of course, she was the Den Mother, and taught a Sunday School class, and was involved in the Crippled Children whenever I went to a special school. She pushed me into schools, sometimes into regular classes. When that was impossible, she taught me herself at home. We read the same books and became disillusioned with the Christian Church for the same reasons. I got my pointer, talking board, and typewriter when I was eighteen and turned out to be a political radical, with socialist ideas, and Mom followed along as far as she could and still be married to a military man.

Dad accused her of brainwashing me. People always did that. Whenever I had an idea, got a good grade, or a merit badge, people gave her most of the credit as if she did the work for me. It was hard to tell where I ended, and Mom began. Even for me, it was hard. Every time before when I moved away from home, moved away from her, there were still strings, seemingly forced on us by welfare … things like her getting my check. The strings undermined my freedom, my own life. They pulled me back home, back under her shadow. We could have probably broken the strings. But it was too easy for me to let her help. However, when she said I was undesirable, something snapped. I was on my own

CHAPTER V – PART 2

It was like standing on a cliff on a cold, windy night … looking up and seeing the stars … then looking down and knowing you have to jump or be turned into salt. I had to live my own life my own way from now on.

The same thing snapped years before when were stationed in Morocco. I saw how my friends, the Arab Beggars, went through the trash cans looking for things to eat, and how they went to the bathroom squatting in the empty field across the road. I wanted to help them, especially the beggar boy who brought his monkey to do its tricks for me for free. Being eight, I had nothing with which to help them … except Jesus. I love Jesus. If they only knew about him … that would make their lives a little easier. I had a vision one night. I knew what I was going to do for them.

I could hardly wait until morning to tell Mom of the plan. I was going to rewrite the whole Bible so simply that even the beggars would understand it. Mom just laughed good-naturedly when I told her of my mission. The Bible was already translated into Arabic. I'd better wait until I could write, until I had read the Bible. I got so angry because she didn't take my vision seriously that something snapped, and I ran away from home. When she left the room, I slid out of my chair, rolling or dragging myself to the door, fought the screen door open, and rolled down the walk to the chalk white gate. The gate was open, and I could see the street beyond. Which way should I go on the street? Then Mom came out and carried me back into the house.

This time when the thing snapped inside, I would get through the gate and far down the road before Mom could come out of the house. I had to go places and do things … alone. I would now. I had a new freedom and a new loneliness, stripped of any guilt or sense of duty. If she didn't believe in me, see me, then I didn't owe her anything except to recognize the part, the very important part, she did play in my life. She did play … but no more.

"I'm free! I'm free! And Freedom tastes of reality." But the doubt, the fear, the question, kept going through my head: was Mom right? Only sick girls would want me? Suzy wasn't any proof. She was in her own little, insane world. Only sick girls … sick in their head. Another question followed. Had Mom known before my bladder operation five months ago what the side effect would be? I had found out by myself a couple months later that I was now ninety-five percent safe … thanks to the bladder operation, I couldn't have kids.

No one told me. Maybe no one saw me … maybe everyone was playing a game on me, making me think that I was something, that I was doing something, when they were just playing with me. Either I could curl up into a ball and let them play their games, or I could show them I was working with reality.

PART II THE SECOND VISIT
CHAPTER VI

Moe was feeding me two Big Macs in between waiting on people. The two Big Macs were my breakfast, lunch and dinner, I explained to the college dude who had a hard time remembering what I had spelled. I was not complaining. Moe and I were in the rush season before Christmas ... well, it was supposed to be a rush season ... and Moe was on the go all day, not eating anything (a diet, as Shitface called it), and was looking very shitty. Once a day, he sent a junkie to get the cheeseburgers for me. But I wanted to save Moe, to reveal his plight to his friends so they would help him. Moe was too proud to do it. He came by and shoved another piece of hamburger in me to shut me up. And then moved on to referee a fight between a Jewish father and his frizzy-haired son over an American flag leather jacket.

Daddy would buy the jacket if Son would write the term paper due next Friday at his private high school. He would buy the jacket if Son promised that he'd do it because Daddy trusted Son ... and if Son didn't keep his part of the bargain, Daddy would bring it back. Son wanted the jacket for Christmas and didn't want to write the paper. Finally, after much cursing, Son would maybe write "that fucking paper."

"You've just been bribed, my boy!" said Moe, slapping the boy's back. The old man, who was not going to listen to such language, gave the $60 to Moe.

"I want you home in a half hour to start that paper," Daddy said.

"I'll be there in a little while," Son said as he admired the long fringe.

"I want you there in a half hour."

"In a little while."

As Daddy opened the door, he bumped into someone coming in with a sad-looking hot dog. At first, I couldn't tell if that someone was male or female. Just covering his ears, "he" had brown hair ... brown like his eyes. He looked at me as he took off his plain, wire-rimmed glasses, putting them into his old Army jacket, which was warm but two sizes too big and erased any trace of his figure. He watched Moe give me another bite. Then he said, "Friend, do you want me to feed you?"

It was a chick's voice. She took Moe's place. In between bites, I found out her name was Carol.

"What do you do?" I asked her.

"Nothing."

"You do something. You live."

"Since I got back from California, I've done nothing. Mostly in my room, out of my mother's way. I read. I take Beauregard for walks. Usually we walk to the library, and sometimes we come in here."

The dog, Beauregard, looked like he was about to go within himself permanently.

"I got him from the pound," Carol saw my look. "Someone did something to him; he hasn't forgiven people yet. Doesn't trust people, not even me. But he's coming around with my love. He has to. He needs someone. But I've got to keep him on a leash, or he'd run away from me."

She stopped and went to JT who was talking to Moe. "Excuse me. Friend, but do you have a cigarette?"

"Oh, the old 'friend' trick," JT said as he threw back his hair and gave Carol a cigarette.

She came back and knelt in front of me and lit the Salem. She sat there, looking at me. "Do you need a friend ... someone who will sometimes come in and talk to you?"

CHAPTER VII

I had failed my mission in D.C. I hadn't convinced Moe to drop the store nonsense for a new, free life in Santa Fe. Depression. And the waiting between acts of the Before and After drama. I did not know when and if an act would begin to break the eternal Intermission. People, different kinds of people, kept coming in.

An interesting, unusual person would come in … a person who needed a unicorn to talk to, a mirror to look into to see their inner beauty or who just needed their minds blown a little. I never knew when they'd come. They stood out from the rest who lived their lives automatically. They, the seekers, did not fit with the housewife mothers, plastic hippies going to college to get out of the draft, businessmen who were trying to be mildly hip, spaced-out bikers or the million other roles that the human background takes.

Those individuals who live in the shallow human sea passed me by. They must live that automatic life for a while, maybe all of this lifetime. I float on and in them, this sea. My attention is not on them; it is not focused on them, not yet. I am aware of them, whether I am in the Before and After, or in Sears, or in the college cafeteria. I relate to them. I am in them, with them, I love them. But I did not wait for them, sitting sixteen hours a day, waiting. I was waiting for persons that shoot out at me from the background. Sometimes, many times, I did not know it was happening. Before I started writing this, I didn't even think about it. But I was waiting for those people who needed me to apply the required electrical push, to send them on their way into what they had to do. Waiting for people who would do the same thing for me. Waiting, most of the time, for when another person and I could do this thing for each other at the same time. Waiting for an opening of energy between me and another person, an opening that would literally change the history of Man. Such an opening could be so absurd a situation that nobody would believe it; or it could be so small, so natural, so fast, that it was beyond us both. But this was what I waited for. I couldn't lie down for very long, even to piss, for fear of missing energy openings. I had already read all the issues of Zap Comics and Rags, so now I just sat there under the waiting.

"Yes," I answered Carol, "And someday could you take me to the library?"

"What do you read?"

"Everything. What do you read?"

"Mostly about God. There is nothing else to do."

Carol looked bored. "Man has to give his life to God, and only by that can he change the world. It is getting late, and I have to fix dinner. I'd like to come back and talk some more and take you to the library. Not tomorrow, though. I've got to drive my brother to the air base ... He's going to Germany, and the day after, Mom wants me to go to a wedding of one of her friends, get into a dress and listen to them talk about dull things. I'd rather talk to you. I'll be back soon."

Carol pulled on the leash, telling Bo, shivering in the corner with fright, that it was time to go, and disappeared into the cold winter night's air.

CHAPTER VIII

Being down in the city could be fatal, literally fatal. I must maintain my Santa Fe high. So, I sang with the record player overhead in the tower. That was what I did all my life. Whenever I was sad, and horny, lonely, rejected by chicks, empty, I'd ask to be lain down in my room with the record player or the radio on full blast. Alone, I'd sing with the music ... moving around the bed dancing, being the lead singer on stage. By being totally free in that way, I got rid of the pent-up feelings and energy. At first, I had to be alone to do this.

When someone was listening, I'd tense up and the sounds wouldn't come. What do they think; do they think that my sounds are awful, or do they think I'm crazy? These were my thoughts when I wanted to sing along with the car's radio. I would start, but something blocked me. In high school, I broke through something and sang along whenever I felt like it, ignoring people when they asked, "Do you want something?" or "What's the matter?" Weird. I couldn't talk, but I could carry the melody when the radio was on, or at rock concerts where no one else could hear me. I couldn't sing by myself. I always wanted to ask the speech therapists about this, but never did.

Magical Mystery Tour was on. The people in the shop didn't know that I was the lead singer beckoning them.

"All aboard for the Magical Mystery Tour! Step right this way!"

It was me, "Day after day, alone on a hill, the man with the foolish grin keeps perfectly still. Nobody wants to know him. They can see that he's just a fool and he never gives an answer. But the fool on the hill sees the sun going down, and in the eyes in his head, sees the world spinning around."

I was always the singer, always the deejay too. Had a few hits. Do you remember "Tennessee Waltz"? That was my first hit. Worked in Dayton, Ohio; before that, sang "On a Bicycle Built for Two". I exercised my legs on the bed. After trying to get Kellogg's Sugar Pops off the bed into my mouth with my tongue. I wasn't satisfied with those songs. So, I went to Morocco for two years to study the Arabic music. Weird flowing sounds come from human guts. But it didn't feed me, so I got a job in the Armed Service Radio in Casablanca. Between radio shows like The Breakfast Party, Ozzie and Harriet, The Green Hornet, Fibber McGee and Molly, and the classical and jazz shit, I sang my songs. At first it was things like "Rockin' Robin" and "Rock Around the Clock". It was better, but still my songs were missing something.

"Well on the way, head in a cloud, the man with the thousand voices talking perfectly loud. But nobody ever hears him or the sound he fears to make, and he never seems to notice."

When I sang "You are Nothing But a Hound Dog", it made a change. 'They' were still writing the songs that I sang, and 'they' were still hiring the band and the singers to back me up. But 'they' allowed me sexual image and I expressed the real feelings of The Teenagers.

I was a smash, the biggest thing to hit the world ... I was hired by the radio station KLO in Salt Lake City and Ogdon, Utah. I signed a nine-year contract. At first, I did good shit like 'Jailhouse Rock', 'King Creole', 'Wake Up Little Suzy', 'Suzy Q', but at the end of nine years, 'they' were having me do things like 'Splish Splash', 'One

Eyed One Horned Flying Purple People Eater', and 'Teeny-Weeny Itsy-Bitsy Yellow Polka Dot Bikini'.

After the contract ran out, I hid in Germany for two years doing a new show, 'The Stars and Stripes', for the Armed Services radio, but 'they' were still into 1940 soap operas and comedies, canned jazz and boring classical music. Radio Luxembourg finally hired me to do a rock 'n roll show in English every night from seven to midnight. So while the U.S. LISTENED TO THE MUSH BY Fabian, Bobby Ridell and Paul Anka, I was experimenting in Europe.

"And nobody seems to like him. You can tell what he wants to do, and he never shows his feelings."

I came back to the U.S. in '63 to make a different kind of music: 'folk' or what I thought was folk. 'Puff the Magic Dragon', and 'Daddy Let Your Mind Move On'. I wrote these myself.

Out of work. I hid in the piavika Birdcage with a short chick with a tiny mole on her third eye who was in the Blue Grass Band. I demanded the total control over my music. 'They' gave it to me, but 'they' couldn't understand why. My lead was my first real friend, Bill Webb.

Bill wore an old green Army jacket, blue jeans and black stovepipe knee boots. His glasses kept slipping off his babyish face and his brown hair kept growing longer and longer as time went along, which freaked most people out because long hair hadn't come into fashion yet. We got the rest of the band together and called it The Unicorn.

After our first few hits, 'I Want To Be Your Man' and 'She Loves You', we could do anything. With the money that was pouring in, we bought a mansion with a farm where we, the band, could live along with our friends. Our music studio was in the attic, and we had a nightclub in the basement where we sometimes played for our friends. Sometimes we charged money that we gave to the civil rights and the peace movements. I always had a reason for being in the group. To meet a lot of people worth knowing. That was the fun about being me. It was fun jamming with all of those people, melting them into the group, into the Unicorn.

Our always changing was the secret of all our hits. I picked people who had a lot of talent. While they were developing their talent in the group, they made The Unicorn grow and change. When they matured enough to think- or to know- that they could make it on their own, they left The Unicorn, returning sometimes just to jam. The back-up group kept changing for the next two years, but I, as the lead singer, and Bill, as the lead guitarist, remained the focal point for the group. Then, in the summer of '66, Bill split to San Francisco to do a folk protest gig. I wanted to go too, but I was under contract to 'they', who built a bigger studio to ease my sadness. I found another lead guitarist, but I wasn't close to him like I was to Bill.

"He never listens to them. He knows they are the fools. They don't like him."

Alone again. I had the group, The Unicorn, but I wasn't close to them. So, I started rebuilding the band. Finally, during the winter of '67, The Unicorn was the way I wanted it. It was our best year under 'they' with acid rock. We were a queer-looking band, but we were close to one another. For a short while, we changed our name to Sgt. Pepper's Lonely Heart's Club Band, but we changed right back to The Unicorn.

We were a queer-looking band to 'them', but we loved one another, and we loved our fans. We were close; that was the important thing. There was Phil DeWitt, the lead guitarist. Hitler would have been proud of Phillip, outwardly the ideal of the master race. Blonde crewcut and pink skin. He was a tall, skinny scarecrow with blue dreamer's eyes who, when he was in his suit, could con any store clerk. But when Phil wasn't on his straight looking trip, he went around unshaved and in rags. Phil was from the planet Slarnis. So was one of the band's chicks – the chick with the two names, Diane and Grace (I never knew which one was her real name and which one she was a going by at that moment). There are a lot of freaky beings on earth who are from Slarnis.

CHAPTER IX

On Slarnis, there are three islands: Sedes, Locian and Lemlops.

On Sedes, where Diane-Grace came from, the people have no identity except for their names. They have learned the value of silence as a communication media. Sedesians have no personality walls. They don't use words as filters to screen in what they really mean or feel or to hide what they really are. With silent projections, they must be totally honest. If they aren't totally honest, their projections will boomerang the dishonesty back into the dishonest Sedesian's body, where it will be trapped in the joints. The more that a Sedesian is dishonest, the more the body aches as he grows older. Eventually, dishonesty could be fatal on Sedes. But most Sedesians are young and flexible because they avoid dishonesty. Rather than being dishonest, they express even 'evil' thought, through the medium of silence. Then, you can feel exactly where a Sedesian is at, but they are always changing ... extremely quick changing.

The people on Locian, where Phil came from, are very verbal. But when they speak to you, they take you to some place. Their words don't take you anywhere. Locian words are pretty pictural sounds that have no meaning, no substance. On Earth, people usually love, but don't trust Locians. To Earth, Locians seem to be lazy, shiftless and are not to be given any material responsibilities. But the earthlings listen to the Locians to be carried away into imaginations. The earthlings walk away from the word creators, confused, thinking strange thoughts which did not come from their own brains, and dream for nights afterwards of places they know they belong, of places where something inside of them went when they were talking to a Locian. The mischievous Locians are usually con-men dreamers, carnies and poets when they come to earth with their mind-reading ability.

I came from Lemlope, the middle island on Slarnis. Lemlope is uninhabited except by a priest caste. In the fourth month on Slarnis, the Sedesians pick a young woman and the Lociens pick a young man. They court and mate on the plain of Lemlope. When a child is born, the couple are sent back to their islands and the child is raised by the priests. The Lemlope children have balanced the qualities, traits and powers of both the Sedesian and the Locian cultures. I was a child of Lemlope.

Each child of Lemlope has his own mission. The Unicorn's mission is to bring the earth into love through music. Through the silent communication of Sedes, we convey to our listener a hidden truth that is so simple, that it can't be put into earth words openly. The listener can sense the total Sedesian honesty that the band projects; but the listener's brain can't rationalize or analyze that honesty. It is just there. With the Locian word, energy, played through this band, the insides of the listeners are transported to the gardens of mansions where they dream. The band pushes the listeners into living their dreams in reality.

That was the band then. Just before I had come to D.C. this second time to jam with Moe and the Before and After, I was singing in Santa Fe on my commune. We sang country rock. "We are the hippy, gypsy, peacenik, fearless, trucking, lovin', praying keepers of the Dream. We'll be the farmer peasants. Sit back and enjoy the present."

There was a lull, and Moe came over to give me a hit of orange juice from the carton.

CHAPTER X

OK. OK. You can pray for me. But let go of my hand so I can dance. I don't mind you kneeling on the dance floor, surrounded by moving bodies, praying to your God about me. I can use all the positive thoughts I can get. But I won't stop having a gas just to fit the sad character you need to pray for. You follow me around like a teenybopper following a rockstar. Waking me up late at night to tell me of your dream.

Jesus told you that if you came to me and placed your hands upon my head, centered or focused all your faith towards me ... directed it to me through your hands ... you could heal me. And here you are again. OK. You can put your hands on my head. The last time you focalized the prana energy from your third eye by placing a crystal rock on 12 places on my body. That time you took too long with your rituals, and I had to kick you out of my room because I had visitors coming. Now do what you have been told to do. Every time we go through this, I wish I could fulfill what you wish to do. I really feel guilty when I don't get up walking and talking. I want to walk and talk for you so your faith will not get shattered when you fail to heal me.

Why do you put your God through such needless tests? Needless because I am already healed. I was healed a long time ago by someone who accepted me the way I was before the change. He healed me because I couldn't do what I had to do then without a normal body. Now it's different. I have to have this body to do what

I now have to do. I couldn't do it with a normal body. But the basic principle of healing is the same. You have to accept and love what you are healing … really loving and accepting. Now go back to bed … or read the Bible to find out why I didn't walk away with my bed.

When Moe carried me out to my spot in the front of the store one morning, something was waiting for us.

"Oh! That poor boy! Does he take vitamins? He should, you know. If he took vitamins, he would walk. There is a vitamin for every part of the human body! That is what Doctor Heamoff says."

"Is that a fact?" said Moe, while the frizzy, redheaded old woman pulled out a diagram of the male body with arrows connecting each vitamin to a different part of the body with a short description of the effects.

"What was the diagnosis?" the woman, peering over her glasses at me, asked in a hushed tone.

Oh come on, anyone up there … have a heart! This is just too early for something like her. I haven't had breakfast yet. But OK.

"The diagnosis is Cerebral Palsy … with a slight case of dope addiction," Moe answered the bag of bones who thought she was a health expert.

"He doesn't really take drugs, does he?"

"Mother, he's just kidding you," quietly said the primly dressed young woman who stood behind the old powerhouse.

"I do take dope."

"Shame on you! You should take vitamins instead! C, B, B2, A … they are the basics. You should take them every day. I can get them for you if you give me the money. I will get them at the weekly meeting with Dr. Heamoff. And I'll ask him for the vitamins which will make you walk and talk."

"Now Mother!"

"The only thing that will cure him is SEX," Moe said.

"Sex and drugs won't do anything for him. If you would only give him vitamins ... and cut his hair ... then he would be normal."

"What does his hair have to do with his walking?" Moe asked.

"Why don't you take care of him better ... giving him drugs, not giving him what he needs, not cutting his hair?"

"But he doesn't want his hair cut. Why don't you ask him what he wants?" Moe suggested.

"No, I don't want my hair cut," I said.

"But it is so dirty," Mother said.

A girl of about fourteen came in the store, took one look at me and cried, "Exhibitionist!" She marched up to Moe and demanded to know how he could use a human, even if I was a cripple, in that way. Then she ran out crying. By that time, the old lady had pulled a brush out of her purse and was approaching my head ... which would have been all right with me except that I had not washed it since I arrived at the store due to the lack of a bathtub. My hair was one big, gummy knot. She had only to look at it to renew her attack on Moe.

CHPATER XI

Fuck it. You took me for rides in your old blue Ford. Took me for rides. I was wondering how I would get back to Santa Fe. Getting to D.C. was a miracle. I could not get on the plane. We tried three times to sneak me on the plane alone. The last time was done with full fanfare suitable for a notable who I am. My press agent, hired for me by Universal Pictures, made the arrangements over the phone. He explained to the airport's public relations manager that I was a handicapped film writer with Universal whom Dennis Hopper brought to New Mexico to work on a new movie. But now I had to get to the nation's capital to sign a contract which meant thousands of dollars to me. The airport's PR promised I would get the red carpet treatment when I arrived with my two aides. Everything went fine … I dug playing the role of VIP. Everything went smooth until we handed in the one ticket before I got aboard the TWA jet. Unfortunately, however, the airport thought the two aides were flying with me. Alone, I became a safety hazard, which was banned from the airlines. I didn't understand the logic of the rule. I was considered to be a danger to the other passengers but if I flew with a frail girl who couldn't do anything for me if the plane went down, I then wouldn't be a safety hazard and could fly anywhere.

Usually, I could get around the rule by asking a fellow passenger to say I was with him. But the physical arrangement of the airports in both Albuquerque and in D.C. made it next to impossible to ask passengers without getting caught by an enraged ticket seller who'd yell at us to stop bothering his clients. Thank God that most of my friends had level heads or some ticket sellers would have had black eyes.

I got to D.C. on the bus after a Mister Peepers appeared going to the same place I wanted to go. Everybody thought Dennis Parson was a FBI agent because, in spite of his old lady worried air and his cloak of kooky yoga and bad-tasting health food, he had a knack of showing up at places where something revolutionary was about to happen and firing questions. But I didn't care what he was. I had to get to D.C. and Dennis was willing to take me on the bus. What did I have to worry about? I only had thirteen lids in my suitcase. But the plane ride would have been much easier. I could have just sat in an easy chair for a couple of hours, watched the clouds and looked down at the table of multi-colored quilt with toy houses, cars, cows, trains and blue ribbons with toy boats running. But no. I had to be trapped in the pay toilet in the Cleveland bus station until Dennis could get another dime ransom to get me out.

But now, how was I going to get back to Santa Fe? Another FBI agent was not likely to pop up to escort me on the bus. I should hope not. We had a hard time getting rid of Dennis when he searched my suitcase and found the dope.

When we arrived at the D.C. bus station, Moe picked us up. Dennis naturally stayed close to us the whole time we were getting into Moe's car. I just told Moe not to open his Christmas presents until Christmas next week. The dope was wrapped in two packages. I thought Moe got the message that Dennis wasn't to be trusted. He took off my pointer and board and folded me into the car, the Honey Bee.

Moe invited Dennis to crash at the store. Dennis accepted saying he wanted to look up an uncle who might put him up and he wanted to find a job in the city. All of this gave me an uneasy feeling because up until he met Moe, Dennis, pushing his glasses up and patting down his hair which he just cut before we started the trip, kept telling me how anxious he was to get back to living on his parents' West Virginia farm. Now he changed his mind. The thing that changed his mind was as soon as we got into the car, Moe started asking me how much grass I brought and how good it was. I sat in between him and Dennis without my board. I shook my head no, I didn't bring any grass … and gave Moe a kick. That's when Dennis decided to "find a job", and when I got more uneasy.

As we drove along through the part of the city that had been burnt in riots and was rebuilt, Dennis asked about the local ashrams and health food stores. Moe did not know about that. But he did know the black people. Sometimes I thought Moe was really only playing being Jewish, was really black inside. He told Dennis exactly why the riots had happened and why there would be riots again.

"I don't believe in violence. The facts are violence can't get anything big or permanent. But if I was black, I would be violent because that would be the only way I could get self-respect."

"But they should not be violent. They should go through channels … then they would get what they want," Dennis said, his nature of being squeamish grandmother showing.

"They have been going through channels for a hundred years and haven't gotten what they think they want … what they were made to think they want. The point is, they don't really want what they think they want … a black kid will, during a riot, smash a store window and take a color TV, but he will leave the set a couple of blocks away. He didn't want the TV at all. He thought he did. But the real reason for his looting wasn't the TV or the excitement of the adventure. For that moment, he felt self-respect because he stood up against everything that put him down. But that self-respect is short-lived, and he starts thinking of himself as a hood and acts accordingly." Moe ended his lecture.

We got to the store finally, and while Dennis was taking a piss in the back bathroom, which smelled of pot and hash as if someone forgot the incense, I told Moe why I kicked him … what our guest's occupation was. Moe sent the word out and made a few calls to cool it. Then he treated Dennis as he would treat a friend who just arrived in town and needed a place to crash. The next day, I started the wheels moving on selling the grass … Dennis had gone to the health food store to get yogurt. I talked to Philip, the pale, skinny hanger-on of the store, about selling for me.

"Sure, I'll look around. But you picked a bad time … JT just got a shitload of good grass. Moe and everybody are selling it. So, it might be two weeks before you can get rid of it. How much do you want for it?"

"Twenty … but I'll take twelve. It's good stuff with only a few seeds and stems."

Phillip shook his head, heavy in thought. But his whole face lit up when I suggested he try a joint. He was about to head into the back room to get one of the two Christmas packages and spend some time in the bathroom with sandalwood incense, but he had to ask, "Why did you carry dope when you were traveling with that creepy FBI guy?"

"What safer way is there? Who would check the bag of a cripple traveling with an FBI agent? I had everything I would need on the trip in a separate sack, so he didn't have any reason to open my suitcase … If that shithead up there," I was looking at Moe working above us at the cash register, "hadn't opened his mouth, Dennis would be gone by now."

As Phillip walked back to get stoned, Dennis walked in the front door with two men in grey coats. One had a trimmed, black goatee. Both of them were straight out of an FBI movie. Their role was to walk behind the superagent. Little Dennis in black glasses didn't exactly fit the superagent, but that is the way it was cast.

Dennis introduced them as his cousins; one of them was supposed to be a business student and the one with the beard was a graduate art student who was interested in getting into commercial art. Moe, unseen by the three on his high perch behind them, made a face as if something was caught under his contacts … as if looking up to heaven in disgust and asking why couldn't they be more original. The three looked around the store very expertly. Doc, warned about Dennis and sitting on one of the car seats trying to read the Quicksilver Times, kept his fox eyes on the trio. After a while, the two relatives told Dennis they would see him later in the day. They left.

Dennis picked up a copy of the local underground paper and then asked Moe if he could use the phone to get a job. Moe had just finished counting yesterday's money, so Dennis took over the tower post. He must have made twenty calls. We who were below listened with great interest. Over the phone he made the rounds of all the points of alternative living in the city … free stores, free schools, radical bookstores, free clinics. What he was doing was finding out what was happening in the city. He wasn't as simple-minded as he appeared. After his calls were over, he marched out of the store, saying he might have a job. Moe, Doc and I just looked at one another.

"He can't be an FBI guyS. He is just too obvious … just too fucking obvious," Doc said, looking like a king in meditation, wearing his long, fur coat and petting his long, red beard with his pale fingers covered with rings.

"That's exactly why he is an agent. He is probably the guy he appears to be. He likes to be around freaks. But he's got all of those patriotic and moral ideas that make him a grandmother. So, he stays on the fringe, just close enough to watch. And he gets information for the FBI to satisfy his grandma ideas of how things are and should be. He is a nice dude for an agent," Moe said and went back to reading The Autobiography of Malcolm X.

Philip came floating out of the bathroom. His glassy eyes told me that he was sold on the product. Moe looked up at the sheepish grin and the half-closed eyes and just said, "I'm glad our new friend took a walk before you tumbled from the opium den!"

"Holy shit, Moe! Was that creep here?"

"With two of his family. Listen, lamebrain, the next time you use the john for time-traveling, use two sticks of incense."

CHAPTER XII

Dennis came back in the early afternoon and started cleaning the store … sweeping the floor, even under the car seats, and dusting off the display of hash pipes and special glass superchargers.

Moe's number one chick, Debbie, was feeding me the usual two cheeseburgers and orange juice. At last Moe had picked one who had a head as well as boobs. She was a solid, down-to-earth person who was studying to be a nurse. But she had one hang-up. She was too neat. She kept wiping away the saliva out of my beard every three seconds. I liked to be clean. But when someone had a thing about not letting the slightest bit of a mess remain, it showed me that the person was too busy worrying about how I look or how he was handling the situation for him just to be with me. Moreover, there was some kind of law that said the more you worry or even think about the mess, the bigger the mess gets. I slobber gallons more when I or someone else worries about it. But Debbie was too solid not to get over that fast, especially around Moe, who never did give a shit about that sort of thing. She had to get over it to be the nurse that she wanted to be.

I was sitting, looking at the wall of clothes that separated the back room from the main part of the store. Two rows of shirts with cartoon characters on the front of them. Daffy Duck. Porky Pig. Road Runner. In between rows and in between shirts, there were enough spaces to see what was happening on the other side. I took a bite and accidentally looked through the shirts.

Dennis was opening my suitcase on my mattress. I watched unseen as he felt around in my clothes in a business-like manner. First, he found the unopened package … it should have been under some brightly lighted tree. He put the package on top of the clothes and picked up a shirt revealing another package. The side of this one had been ripped open … and beside this package laid a Baggie. Philip! You lamebrain!

Dennis didn't even have to look in the opened package. He just put it beside the other one on top of the clothes and stuck the Baggie between the two packages like a baby sleeping between its parents. He didn't close the suitcase but put it under Moe's desk where nobody would notice it … unless they were looking for it. I tipped my head back for another piece of cheeseburger as Dennis walked out of the back room. He called out to Moe that he was taking a short walk. But he would be back to still help clean the place.

"Tell Moe FBI found the dope," I told Debbie.

She went out to get Moe, and they wandered back.

"Did our friend open the wrong present?" Moe asked.

"He would have, but Philip saved him the trouble," I said. "He searched my bag. I saw him, but he didn't see me."

"In that case, how would you like to have a secret mission, my sweets?" Moe asked Debbie.

"I'm game," Debbie said with a gleam in her eye.

Moe put the dope in a brown paper sack and instructed her to go home with the dope in the opposite direction that Dennis had gone and call the store when she got there.

"Yes sir, Captain," Debbie saluted us, gave Moe a long, sexy kiss, and was gone.

Dennis came back in a few minutes and busied himself cleaning the Cerebral Palsy handicrafts display in front. After that, he dusted with great gusto the three Harleys in the middle, under the row of clothes. Suddenly he said in an even tone, "Moe, you've got visitors."

Four big cops came through the door. They weren't the young guys, the regulars on the beat, guys who had just gotten out of the Army or who were in school and needed a job to keep the young wife and the newborn baby in clothes and food. They weren't the ones who came in to get warm, joke with Moe and maybe buy a poster or a blacklight when they got off work. In the Chevy Chase section, where the store was, the cops on the beat worked in twos, one working each side of the street. Obviously, these guys wanted something more than to warm their feet.

"We'd like to look around," said the fattest, the most bored one of the foursome.

"Sure. Knock yourself out." Moe said good-naturedly. The phone started to ring. Moe cried, "Got it!" and scrambled up the steps of the tower. He stopped long enough to tell the cops, who were filing into the back room, that they should make themselves at home. They mumbled for a few minutes among themselves. Moe called down from the tower to tell them they could see the posters better if they turned on the overhead blacklight.

Soon they marched out, saying they would be back when they had enough money to buy the "EARTH … THIS IS GOD … YOU HAVE THIRTY DAYS TO CLEAR OUT … I HAVE A CLIENT INTERESTED IN THE PROPERTY" poster.

When they had left, Dennis came up next to Moe and knowingly asked, "Were they the Vice Squad?"

"What would the Vice Squad want here? I always get the age of the chicks I sleep with. Other than that, I am a healthy, legal male."

"But still, people have to be careful," Dennis said with an undercurrent of an attempted threat … as much a threat as a mouse could master against a lion.

"Nah. You see, I got a letter yesterday asking me to write on my highest ambition. I wrote them that my highest ambition is to live until I am a hundred. That's my main purpose … the only goal for living. Anything else that happens to me is pure gravy."

"But the way I figure it, I won't hit the century mark by worrying or by being careful. I don't give a shit what happens to me. If it is shit, I can handle it; if it is putting out along the highway, I dig it. But either way, I am living," Moe said. And added to me, "That was Debbie on the phone. She says she hopes you stay around for awhile because she wants to get to know you … or some such shit."

Next morning, Dennis decided that he should work on his folks' West Virginia farm after all. There were some real nice people in the town near there. A little straight … a little narrow … but real good people. We all … the Before and After crew … let out a sigh and raced into the bathroom after Dennis left. All except Moe, the straight freak, and me, who had to wait until closing time to get stoned.

Even if Dennis was a milk toast agent, he did get me to D.C. And FBI agents don't always pop up when you need one. I would have to get back home without the help of an agent. So how was I getting back? How in the fuck did I know? Again, I would have to wait for a key to come to me.

CHAPTER XIII

You must be awake when the key comes. Stretching away out, out … go catch it, grabbing hard. When you have caught the key, you have to search for the right lock.

The lock that you tried to break is rarely the one that you really wanted open. You find that out when you catch the flying key.

Then you have to go down the hall under the rabbit hole, trying the key in every door you come to. The key comes to you, but then you have to work to use it, to make it matter at all.

When you come to the right door, the key turns into a light blue magic carpet. There is a trick to using this carpet … knowing when to lie back and let the magic carpet take you where it will, and when to force it by your will to take you where you desire to go …

Sometimes the carpet will just hover over one place if you don't use your will. You will be trapped ninety feet in the air. But you don't know the terrain. You have traveled this way a long, long time ago once, and have a vague idea where you want to go.

I was waiting for that key that would turn into a magic carpet that would take me to Santa Fe. And Carol, with her dog, Bo, came in bearing a box of home-made brownies and a fruitcake.

"Marry her!" Moe advised me when he saw the food. But he wouldn't take a bite no matter how Carol tried to force a brownie into his mouth. He was on one of his week fasts. Drinking only chocolate milk and orange juice, he thought he was keeping fit. And at the end of the week, he would have an eating contest.

After Carol saw that Moe was both illogical and impossible, she pushed me outside to take a walk around the block to get away from a high school kid who somehow got the idea that Carol had some grass. She had gone to the wedding and had driven her brother to catch the plane to Germany. Now she had his car ... or at least she had it when her mother didn't get the whim to keep it in the garage until he came back three years from now.

The key. The magic carpet. She was like a princess locked in a tower and under a spell. She would slowly turn to stone, getting more and more rigid.

"I want to get back to my home, but I don't have any way to get back. I do have money."

Drive me. Take a risk. You are doing nothing here playing your guitar in your room ... driving in the city where there is no place to go, walking that paranoid dog who can't decide which side of the chair he wants to walk on. I wouldn't live like that. I couldn't. There was a time when I was living at home with my folks, and was going to college, that I wanted to go insane so I could hide in front of the TV without thinking that I should be doing more. I couldn't figure out the trick of going insane. I saw many people doing it, and it looked simple enough. But I just couldn't do it to save my life. I kept wanting sane things such as living away from home in a commune where there were many people so that I could live not depending on one person. One person can die, and where would I be then? That was the boat I was in then. My parents were getting old. When they died, where would I be ... even if I kept getting straight A's and got my PhD, I still would have to go to a rest home or a mental institution or to somewhere where the human vegetables are. Staring at a TV if I was lucky, staring at a bone white ... cracked ... stained ... ceiling if I wasn't lucky, for the rest of my life. My body would probably live long after I was gone. The more I learn, the more ideas I had, the more awareness I achieved, the bigger the bottomless pit there would be when I was finally forced into bed in front of the TV. I was working against myself, working so hard to be the real me, to learn things, to do things with people, pushing myself into them. One part of me kept looking down at what I was doing, saying and laughing, "You fool! Slow down so you won't get whiplash when you smash into that stone wall. You better take some morphine so you won't feel the shock when the rug is pulled out from under you. Kill yourself. Well, you might not be physically capable of killing your body, but you can kill your mind … your spirit." The only problem was that I couldn't turn my mind off or kill my spirit. I had gone too far into living for that. One of my friends talked to me about taking acid so that I could live in a spaced-out state where nothing could bother me. I could lie in bed and groove. Sounded great. But nobody would give me anything stronger than hash. When I was trapped into living until the end. I could keep on doing what I had been doing … going to college and living at home, having friends who wouldn't go beyond a certain point with me. I could have done that and waited for my doomsday, or I could push out blindly in search of a loophole. Taking risks. I didn't see them as risks because anything would be better than doomsday. I am not anything different than you. My problems, fears and doubts aren't any bigger or littler than yours. I am the same as the guy who had to decide to get a job that he doesn't like so he can live or turn to start hitching into the unknown. My life is more clear-cut, more obvious. Knowing that doesn't soothe my aches, smooth my way any. Just makes me see an ache as an ache, not a human crucifixion. A hill as a hill, not an impassable mountain. What I am asking you to do is take a risk. Drive me to Santa Fe. I will buy a car for you. When you get there, you can see what's happening there. On the way you might start to see me. Once there, you can decide if you will stay. Or you can go on to see your friends. The car will be yours. You could even turn around and come back to D.C. I hope you won't do that. I am beginning to see what D.C. is doing to you. But if you don't see what D.C. is when you get to Santa Fe … well, I will be wrong. I know you can't decide tonight. And I know we will have to wait until your brother sends the deed from Germany.

CHAPTER XIV

She said she would think about it. We got back to the store and Carol said she had to leave to cook dinner for her mother and brother. She left and Moe shouted from the back room "Are you still hungry? I made my special … egg on toast. It's a shame that I am on a diet."

"You have bookkeeping work to do. I'll feed him," said Debbie, taking the plate from him and coming to the front.

Debbie said to me in a quiet tone so she would not be overheard, "How did you ever get close to him … really close? I've been trying to get close to him, but every time that we almost get there, he throws a fucking wall up … makes a joke and puts his he-man shit in front of him."

Debbie was different than most of Moe's chicks. In college, they would come to me sitting in the noisy cafeteria and ask the same two basic questions: "What does he really think of me?" and "How can I get him to marry me?" I always got the Dear Abby questions. Ever since I got my board and pointer, I have been put in the role of Advisor.

Really, I just bullshit my way through questions, using what I've read or seen … seen from watching people. And people believed in my bullshit, my advice.

The amazing thing was that it usually worked for them. It didn't work for me. With Moe's would-be wives, there was nothing there except a good time for a few nights. They didn't have what it would take to tame him. It would have taken a women to do that. And they were chicks. But Debbie was asking something different.

"I just don't pay any attention to the wall. I can bullshit as much as he can … but I see what he needs from me … and I force it onto him, ignoring what he says," I said.

"But he says he doesn't need anybody except himself," Debbie said.

"Do you really believe that?"

"Well, he is a strong guy."

"Sure, he is strong. But he is afraid of testing his strength by letting people give to him."

Moe was always giving to people. That was why he was so popular in college. He fit in the frat crowd as well as the freak scene because he was always giving in whatever terms the situation called for. But the moment that someone got close enough to him to really give him something, he would hop on his motorcycle with his buffalo horns on and ride alone into the sunset where freedom is supposed to be.

Moe was a master giver. But giving only took him halfway into freedom and then trapped him in his own strength. He had only himself … he wasn't dependent on anyone … it was all right that people leaned on him. That proved that he had his shit together. But he didn't trust people enough to depend on them, to let them give to him. Me, I just sneaked in when he wasn't looking and as he was busy giving to me, I was giving to him in an underground way. I couldn't give Moe all that he needed … just what was in me.

Somewhere along the line, I had learned to give up feeling guilty about always taking, always receiving and seeing I was not giving anything in return … it seemed like I wasn't giving. I didn't want to depend on people. I wanted to be independent, just giving to them.

But that kind of independence, that kind of freedom, was impossible for me. I had to depend on people to make my living. A simple thing like depending on people to not leave me lying in a bed in a room with a closed door … forgetting me forever … me dying of thirst in my own shit and piss. People wouldn't do that to me. They may leave me for hours and I may have to piss my pants. But in the end, they will come back and put dry pants on me. If that was the only level of my life – waiting, drinking, pissing and shitting – I still would be forced to depend on people. But as it is … how I am and how my life works, I have to take it for granted that people will be there giving. And they always are.

I sometimes felt guilty because I was using people … they gave me so much. Then I made two discoveries. The first one was the Art of Receiving … that when you let someone do something for you, giving something to you, letting him in the right way, in the way that makes him feel warm inside, you are giving him something in return, usually of more worth. And the second discovery was that everyone was just as dependent on others as I was in bed. But they didn't know it, didn't want to know it.

Moe could deny it. He could say he didn't need anyone else … that he had it together, that he could go it alone and do what he wanted to do alone, that he was quite happy, thank you. When someone came into the room where I had been lying for six hours alone and asked me if I wanted to get up or take a piss, I could have said, "No." I could have said no out of pride, not wanting to admit that there were things, that I would deserve to die in my own shit. But I could also have said no because I didn't want to be a bother, because I was not sure if the person who came in really wanted to help me. This would be equally absurd.

But I had done this many times … out of false pride … but deeper, because I didn't trust the person … didn't trust that he really wanted to help me … thought he was doing it out of some kind of duty ... or maybe he was angry that I pissed on the bed ... maybe he didn't really love me. So I would say no.

But this time Moe was in bed, and Debbie and I were standing in the door. We could believe him when he said no, when he said he could do things himself. We could walk out and close the door like people did before us ... or we could trick him into letting us help him ... trick him in such a way that he wouldn't realize that he was being helped until afterwards, too late for him to put up the wall of pride ... too late for him to feel trapped.

CHAPTER XV

It was about closing time. Buzzy, another of the Before and After crew, came in and sat down beside Debbie on the bottom step of the tower.

"It's a slow night at Bimbo's, so I decided to come here and crash," Buzzy said, wiping his black hand on his Daffy Duck shirt. "Phillip just got a letter from the Merchant Marine school. He is going up to New York next week to get his physical. Hey Moe!"

Moe walked slowly out from the back room, switching off the lights and locking up. Another day of Before and After was about to end.

"Your old man knows somebody high up in the school, doesn't he?" asked Buzzy.

"Yeah, the president."

"Could your old man pull some strings to get me in?"

"Anything to get you out of here. I'll call him tomorrow."

"What's with him. Used to be he wore bright clothes … bellbottoms, of course … and go on dates. A real swinger," Buzzy said.

"He was fun when he came in the store … so light," Debbie said.

"Then dear Mother came home. Back into grey clothes … and he's getting fat," Moe said.

"He doesn't seem happy anymore," Debbie said.

"Mother fooled all of us," Moe grunted as he lifted me and carried me to the back room to lay me down on my mattress. I never figured out why he didn't just roll the chair into the room. Guess he wanted to prove his strength. Men always did that kind of thing.

Buzzy spread two blankets on the floor beside the mattress and stripped off his clothes ad Moe undressed me. Then Moe carried his roll of blankets to the other side of the multi-colored wall of clothes.

You never could get Moe to sleep in a real bed even when there was on handy ... even a mattress was not his style. It freaked Mary, his folks' black maid, when she came to work at the three-story white house in Georgetown and found Moe ... Jeff to her ... sleeping nude on the living room rug. But there was many a girl who was willing to sleep on the floor for him. Debbie did that night.

"Ah yes! Before and After ... the only clothing motel!" Buzzy chuckled in the W.C. Fields tone and turned out the blacklight.

During the night, I woke up for awhile. The bathroom light was left on. Debbie walked by on her way there. Nude, white body with proud breasts ... not overbearing giants ... just proud. I was used to nude bodies ... but I wondered if I would ever get a girl. I went back to sleep a little sad.

CHAPTER XVI

Every morning was like a dressing room on a movie sound stage. Moe picked our costumes out of stock. Usually things that he had too many of and wanted to sell. People would buy anything they've seen you wearing. The shirt that, if they'd seen on the rack, and thought was ugly, the shirt they hadn't given a second look, would be practically ripped from your body. They would beg you to sell your shirt ... if they loved you. So we dressed up every day for our audience.

My costume of the day before either went into my suitcase for my fashion-coordinated wardrobe or into the wash to be put back on the rack. We were in our new costumes ... a ruffled shirt that sold four years ago for thirty dollars when JFK wore them instead of wearing ties. After he was shot, you couldn't give them away. They were so ugly ... like something a gay intern would wear. Moe took them off the Manufacturer salesman's hands for fifty cents apiece, and was trying to sell them for a dollar. Good luck!

Anyway, we got dressed and went out front to meet the early afternoon sun through the door. Moe went through the ritual of starting up the store ... opening the door to let the tropical heat out ... putting on Tommy by the Who and putting one of the speakers outside the door to attract attention ... switching on the lights and putting the five phones back on the hooks. I didn't appreciate having the phone on the desk over my head ringing me awake. So every night, Moe would make the necessary precautions. As soon as he put the phone back on the hook, it started ringing.

Moe picked up the receiver and cheerfully said, "City Morgue … you kill 'em and we'll chill 'em."

Must have been the hotline … Alfred calling from the Silver Spring store for the daily strategy. Then the other phone rang.

"Hey Shitface," Moe peered over the tower wall down at me. "Are you in and taking visitors? That was Suzy on the phone. Remember, your old chick from the first visit? She's in town and she said she's coming right over to see you."

CHAPTER XVII

Suzy appeared during my first D.C. visit; she was lonely, caught in this world. But she couldn't be of this world. She would shatter if she had to stay here much longer.

It was hard to believe she was really real. Really a flesh and blood person. More like a sad spirit with pale, oval face with large, black eyes which went back for ages upon ages. I fell into them when I first saw her sitting on the tower step, just listening, just watching from somewhere far inside herself. Her hair was the only part of her that was happy. Long sunbeams, now red, now yellow. The sun of her hair surrounded the moon of her face. Pale, white milk with streaks of blue. Her hands were like a child's, with long, fragile fingers. Her body was so fragile, I was afraid she would blow away, vanish into the nothingness where she had come from. She just sat there on the step, bundled up in an old navy coat, looking sadly at me.

"What is your name?" I pointed out on my board. I knew she read it and understood it. She was not ignoring me. She wanted to answer me, but the words would not come out. Her lips moved a little, trying to form words. But she remained mute. Just sitting there looking sadly sad.

[*Editor's note:* There are some missing pages here.]

"See me! Feel me! Touch me! Heal me!" Debbie and Buzzy were straightening up the bellbottoms, stacking them neatly into the cubbyholes along the left store wall. Moe was talking to a middle-aged woman who fell in love with the shirt he was wearing.

"I want three of these darling shirts for my son," she said, clinging to Moe's arm, feeling the texture. "How much?"

"For you, three dollars for three. What taste you have!"

Three down. I looked through the window, and there was Suzy smiling at me. She ran in and hugged me, then she sat on the car seat just like the year before … wearing the same clothes she wore the last time … now they were pinned together in danger of falling apart at any minute. She had changed.

"You are getting fat," I said. She looked healthier, less like a ghost.

"I am not," Suzy said smiling.

Wait a minute! She talked! She talked in a low, breathless tone which I could hardly hear. But she talked. She didn't need my board anymore. It looked like that smile, that silent laugh last year, had caught hold and spread. Suzy came out of her world finally …even if she didn't come to the coast. I had waited for a week last year; then when she didn't come, I got worried. Maybe she had been caught in the rescue attempt. So I had called Moe. He said she had been in once since I left. When he asked when she wanted to take the plane ride, she just stared into space and went blank. That was the last time I heard anything of her. She disappeared. But now her Southern drawl made me laugh. Her voice made her so sexy, so coy in spite of herself. However, something kept running through my head: Why didn't you come? I didn't want to ask that. It wasn't fair to ask that because it would come out like an accusation … there wasn't anything to accuse Suzy of. She didn't know what I went through because of her. What I went through gave me more freedom. So I didn't mind. But the question wouldn't go away.

"Because you were here with me," Suzy answered.

"I was with you in thought."

"That isn't what I mean. I didn't have to because you were here. You didn't leave me. I talked to you every day. We hitched to places together. Don't you remember?"

"You were here with me in my world," Suzy said, and added with a little ironic smile, "If you were in California, why didn't you write me?"

"I didn't know where you were."

"Some excuse!"

Suzy wanted to push me around the block, so Debbie got me into my coat and showed Suzy how to use the brakes. When we got through the door, Suzy halted like she had forgotten something. She went back into the store without me. I braced my feet on the sidewalk and turned around to see what was happening. Suzy went back and forth in and out of the door as if the cameraman took the same shot over and over again, as if Suzy was trapped in walking out the door. The unlocked wheelchair wanted to roll down the hill, but my feet stopped it. After Suzy walked through the door for the twentieth time, she resumed pushing me as if nothing out of the ordinary had happened. It was a sunny, but chilly day. The ice had melted from the sidewalk so it was an easy ride. Suzy stopped and left me again. My feet went automatically down. Suzy went back a couple of feet and it looked like she was talking to someone. I couldn't hear her words. Moreover, I couldn't see the person she was talking to. There was nobody there. She was trying to coax the person to come along with us, pulling on his coat sleeve like a young girl trying to pull her tired grandpa to the candy store. Finally, the invisible old gentleman consented and let Suzy lead him by the hand, over to me. We continued our walk … the three of us. But the old fellow kept lagging behind and Suzy kept going to get him. Suzy was in a happy air, skipping over the sidewalk cracks. But she wouldn't walk inside of telephone signs. When we came to one of those, she would leave me, walk in the street past the pole, then return to the walk and come back for me. At this rate, it took us an hour to walk around the block. If Suzy did this all of the time, I wondered how she escaped being picked up like she was before … or at least avoided attracting attention. I enjoyed our normal walk, even though I was back in the horror movie. The Invisible Man.

When we were back in the store again, I asked, "Who was walking with us?"

"Just someone I once knew."

"Is he dead?"

"I don't know. Maybe. He is past," Suzy said, then hugged me and left. At least, she tried to leave. She was walking out and the door got in her way again. She kept going in and out, opening and closing the door, waving her hand in her face as if she was trying to take in some of the store's good vibes, splashing them in her face, wrapping them around her to protect her while she was away from the store. After one last ring of the bell over the door, she was gone.

"Does she always do that?" I asked Debbie, who was watching the ritual too.

"Most of the time, at least around here where we accept her … sometimes she seems to forget and goes through a doorway just once … but not often."

"It's a wonder she gets anything done or goes anywhere that way. She is talking again; I thought she was better. But she is worse."

"Suzy is strange. But I like her. It just takes getting used to walking with her invisible friends."

"I found that out," I said.

Later that day, Carol came in with Bo to push me to the library. When we got there and tied the dog just inside of the first glass door, Carol asked what kind of book I wanted.

"Something on witchcraft and magic," I said.

"Why on earth do you want to read something like that?"

"There is a girl who comes into the store … pretty freaked out. Her whole life is twisted around some kind of ritual, based on what she calls "the Curse" that she thinks she is under. Maybe if I invent some magical ceremony and make her believe that it will release her from the whole thing, she will break through it. It's worth a try."

But the library didn't have any occult books. By the time Carol paid a visit to the Religion section, the forsaken Bo was making so much noise we had to hurry to check out the two spiritual books we had, grab the dog and go.

"Would you be up for a ride in the country tomorrow … get away from that place?" Carol asked, pushing me along the sidewalk to the store. "The place is so physical … so material. It is a nice place to go into for awhile to escape. But after a while, it closes in on me. It must close in on you too. That is why I take you on walks … and now with the car, I can take you on rides … maybe take some grass with us."

"Great."

"How can you stand living in that?"

"In what?"

"In the store, with all of that corruption and temptation around you."

CHAPTER XVIII

Traveling along back country roads. Bumps, turns, dips. Each sharp turn pushed me close to Carol, leaning on her. Laughing at the tickle inside our bellies when we went down dips fast.

"These roads are very physical … just like having a back massage, especially with these shocks. Especially when you are stoned. Do you think doing dope is a sin? I am not sure. I see things clearer when I am stoned … that is the way I see things clearer when I am stoned … that is the way I got close to God … through acid. But I should be clear and close to Him all the time without dope. I'm not sometimes … most of the time … and that's the time I take dope … to cover up my weakness. Let me take off my glove … there … let me find your hand hiding in your coat sleeve. I don't want to feel cloth. I want skin! There, isn't that better? Your hand is cold. When we get back to the store I'll give you a back massage … ever had one? I love to give them … playing with skin, giving people pleasure. I drive on these roads, just Bo and me. But I like to talk to someone when I am driving. That's why I like you so much … I can talk to you and you really understand. Are you uncomfortable like that?"

During her monolog, I had slipped down so that my head was laying on her belly, a soft pillow … but her elbow kept jabbing me every time we made a turn and my back was getting a little strained, falling half off the seat. She stopped the old Ford and sat me up, popping my head on her shoulder. Bo was staring jealously at me from the back seat. I was in his place. Come off it! I wasn't going to be a rival to a dog.

We started the car again, after deciding not to roll another joint … that would just be wasting good shit, as high as we were. So Carol lit a cigarette instead. White farm hills dazzled my eyes. White under the bloody sun going down.

"It would be fun driving you to Santa Fe. Being with you all of the way there, but … Look at the sunset! Can you see it? God's painting. We had better get back to the store before you get too cold. I'd better learn how to work the thing in the car before we start the trip … if we do. Getting trapped in a snow blizzard and freezing isn't the best way to go. My father picked the best way … shot himself through the head. I found him in the living room dead. I was rather relieved that he did it … not really, you know. But I was never really close to him. He was always yelling at me, hitting me. He was a very religious man. I guess I'm a lot like him."

I laughed. I couldn't help it. I was sure that he was a very religious man. Beating his kid, shooting himself. Very religious. Carol looked down at me to see why I was laughing. I hoped she wasn't like her old man.

"I didn't have any feelings about his being dead. But I hated him for what he did to Mom by killing himself. Why couldn't he just have run away? We would have understood and forgiven him. But now Mom wonders what she did or didn't do that made him kill himself. That was last year, just before I went out to California."

When we parked in front of the store, Carol went in with Bo to get Moe to carry me all the way to the back room for the massage. Carol had put me into the car by herself to test if she could do it for the trip that she was deciding to make. Getting into the car went smooth … she was strong … but now we were stoned and didn't want to bother with the chair. So two minutes later, Moe danced topless like a drunk prizefighter out of the circus-colored, painted store. He scooped me up with a loud belch in my ear, and carried me to my true love.

Carol was waiting on the mattress to take off my shirt. Moe turned on the overhead blacklight to give that intimate atmosphere. Moe disappeared into the front room where Badfinger was playing. "If you want it, here it is. Come and get it … it may not last!" Red, orange, green and blue day-glo popped out at us from the posters around us. She started scratching my arms and chest … beginning the massage.

"Remember what I told you yesterday about how this store closes in on me and forces me to leave? It is doing that now. I want to stay here with you. A part of me likes this place. I don't feel as comfortable anywhere in the city. Sitting here I can make believe that the city doesn't exist. I feel accepted and comfortable. That part of me wants to stay here … but it's the same part that lusts, stuffs itself with food, wants cigarettes, beer and dope. Why am I so weak? I keep falling into temptation, wanting things of this world … when all I really want is to be spiritual, to give my life. But I keep forgetting."

As Carol sighed, she rolled me over onto my belly and sat on my butt, working the tension out of my back, rocking back and forth.

"I like expressing my love directly like this. The closest I get to a person is when I'm giving him a massage. It is what I like to do the best. I can just feel my love pouring out through my fingers into your back. But sometimes I wonder if it's too sensual."

Carol's voice faded. Her hands guided my body into the relaxed state of half-sleep. Then she gently rolled me over again. Leaning back on the desk leg, she put my head in her lap and softly stroked my face … sometimes she pressed my face to her body. Suddenly she left. I thought she would be back in a minute. I just lay there in a new happiness. No girl before had done just a simple thing with me … holding me tenderly … holding me as if I was a desirable man. It finally dawned on me after lying there for ten minutes that Carol went home.

"Well, Romeo, would you like to join the real world, or are you contented lying there with that idiot grin?" Moe asked, standing over me. "What did you drop, anyways?" I just gave you two birds grass. But that's unmistakably your acid grin."

After Moe put the board on, I asked, "What's with D.C.? Every time I come here, I get involved with a chick."

"We grow loony girls. But I'm still waiting to see you take one home with you."

"That's the trick."

"You'll never do it."

"Want to bet?"

"I'm not a gambler," Moe said, and went back to playing poker on the apple barrel with Lenny, the handsome young blonde who was about ready to quit his hardhat job and join the Before and After crew.

"Gambler he isn't," Lenny said, laying down a royal flush and pulling on his red beard, amused.

"Well, eat me!"

"Now, Captain, remember your blood pressure," Lenny said. "Hey, Mondy, did you hear what your friend Louie pulled off?"

Louie, a cool, Jewish, junkie businessman with professionally styled silver hair, a lot of rings, Moe's most expensive, flashy clothes, and a weasel face – ran a liquor store and sold dope, including smack – "If I didn't do it, someone else would," was what he said when I asked how he could sell heroin --- had something like if you dug about three miles under his surface.

"He painted himself black and put on an Afro-natural wig, and robbed the Riggs bank, just for kicks … almost got away with twenty grand. But three businessmen brought him down with a flying tackle. He smashed his head on the sidewalk and woke up in the hospital," Lenny said.

"He will bribe his way out of it within a week," Moe grunted. "Ah, yes, American justice!"

CHAPTER XIX

The next day, Carol and I went riding again through the grey towns in between the white country and woods of black lines.

"I didn't tell you I was leaving yesterday, but I knew you would understand," Carol said, switching off the crackling radio. "I was so high, felt so good that I had to be by myself, or I'd have melted into you. I walked for a long time with Bo. But where is there to go in this city to be by yourself … without feeling lonely? So I went home and read some of the Bible with Mom. But I couldn't keep my mind on Jesus' words. I kept thinking of you, going back to you. I saw everything you did after I left … really. It must have been telepathy or something. I never felt what I felt coming out of you from anyone else. It is so pure. You're so spiritual."

"Stop the car and give me my board! I am not spiritual … not by your definition of the word. That's a statement of fact. Thank God for that! I am not a saint. I don't qualify for the post. Even if I did, I wouldn't accept the curse because I know how lonely it is. People always put the person who is different from them, who they don't really understand, either above or below themselves. You can't really love someone who is above you. You can worship him, serving him faithfully, blindly. You can fear him, hiding in doubts, avoiding him, leaving him alone. You can hate him, trying to poke holes in his goodness, trying to find his one weakness, one contradiction, one fault with which you can topple him down under your feet. But you can't love the guy above you in a simple human way. To love that way, you must be equals. Only saints are strong enough, foolish enough, to live without receiving that kind of love. I am not a saint. I am a man. See me. But of course, I didn't make her stop the car or her stream of words to see me. Why did she have to put fancy labels on what we did and felt yesterday? It was very simple. We went somewhere together. I didn't know where. Only that we went there together. To say anything more was like denying we ever went. It made everything slightly unreal. We took a ride, got stoned both on grass and each other … I got a massage … we held each other … I fell in love with her, or felt at least something growing between us. That was what happened yesterday. We had a good time … the best time I ever had with someone, especially in the back room … but keep it simple … we had a good time.

"You have a peace and a knowing around you that others can share when they are with you," Carol went on, turning into a rest stop beside the grey Potomac. "That's why I like to be with you. But I can't understand how you can live at the store without becoming like 'them.'"

"Like who?" I asked. She had put my pointer on me and was holding the board in front of me.

"The people who hang out at the store."

"Like you?"

"You know what I mean. They seem to live either for sex or dope. They have no higher awareness. They don't believe in God. But you do, don't you?"

"Yes."

"But how can you when all of that is going on around you? If it was me, I'd fall into man's ways, wanting things. Even now I sometimes doubt God … that he really exists. I know he does because he has gotten me out of places that I couldn't get out of … I thought I could do everything myself ... could handle everything. Until I started hitching around, sleeping on beaches ... Then I ran into things and people that freaked me out so bad that all I could do was lay back and pray, 'OK, God, deliver me, if you're there,' And he did. I would be dead if it weren't for him. But with all of the proof I have, I still doubt, still rebel. Sometimes I want to go wild and say, 'Fuck you, God.' I would too, if I lived at the store. That is what I mean. How do you live in a peace in that chaos?"

"I don't think I live in a peace. But I know the store is shallow. I don't want to live like that ... not for always ... I know there is something more ... I want it. I know I am more. The store can't trap me. I see the good side of the store. I enjoy it. I watch teenyboppers trying to be sexy ... and I am still the same inside ... so I just dig it until it is time to go on."

Carol didn't say anything for a long while ... just smoked her cigarette. Then she crushed it out. "I keep forgetting I'm trying to quit. But I'm cutting down. I don't buy them anymore. Just bum them off of people. Do you love everyone?"

"I haven't thought about it. I don't think that way."

"I thought I could," Carol said. "Before I went to the Coast, I thought I could love everybody because everyone had at least a tiny part that was good, and I could love that part of them. I could see that part when I looked deep into their eyes. I thought that way even when I came back home. I was a mess ... skinny and sick with lice and crabs and no money ... Mom had wired the money for the plane ticket ... it freaked her out to see the state I was in ... I was lucky I wasn't pregnant. Anyway, after I recovered somewhat, I took a walk at around two in the morning in Southeast D.C. I was so naive and innocent. I thought no one wanted to hurt me. A big Negro ... he must have been seven feet and fat ... was standing on the sidewalk. I said hi and walked on. But he grabbed me by the arm and wanted me to have a drink from his whiskey bottle. He was hurting my arm and he was too strong for me to break away. I tried to love him, but when I looked into his eyes, it was hate and evil all the way down deep. He was pure evil. I couldn't love Evil. So I couldn't love him. I should have … That's what Jesus wants me to do … I thought. I've spent most of my time since then in my room … reading."

"Hiding in your room isn't going to change anything," I said.

"I'm not hiding. I'm making myself ready to give my life to Jesus … not just to God, but to Jesus. I don't know quite what that is. But I'm trying to find out because that's what I want to do … That's all there is to do."

"Two guys have tried to kill me," I said.

"Come on! Who would want to kill you?" Carol asked.

"Lots of people. The old drunk who we hired to live with me when I first moved out from home one night beat me up, and then waved a loaded gun at me, threatening to pull the trigger. I was so scared that my body shook all over. I somehow kept yelling and looking straight into his bloodshot eyes. For some reason, he just dropped the police pistol and went to bed, but first he got down on his boy knees beside his bed and prayed."

"The other time was when I was living at the commune in Santa Fe. That night I was sleeping in the Free Store which was carpeted with four inches of old clothes. I was alone, trying to sleep, ignoring the conga drums outside. This biker who had been staying around for a few days, 'helping us out' stumbled in. The Chicanos had beaten him up so many times that his eyeballs were permanently red, which the bottle of Vin Rose didn't help any. When he saw me lying half-asleep on the floor, he picked up a wooden chair and threw it at me. It landed near my head … so near that for the rest of the night I kept bumping my head. Then the guy started playing with his knife and cursing at me, walking towards me. His blonde girlfriend came in, saw what was happening, and pulled him down on the clothes with his head on her breast, explaining to him that I was 'that cripple that don't mean nothin''. He just cried and finally went to sleep."

"That's what I mean," Carol said, "There are people who are pure evil. It's impossible to love them … only Jesus can. I can't, so I avoid them so they won't tempt me."

"Why avoid them?"

"Well, didn't you keep away from the people after you found out what they were?"

"No," I said. "Maybe because I knew what men were like in the first place. So my ideal vision of man didn't explode in my face. People aren't pure … or perfect. Most people are fucked up … more or less. That doesn't mean they're evil … maybe there is no such thing as evil … but I don't think about things like that. I try to see what is real so I don't get clobbered needlessly or miss some beautiful spark. I am just bullheaded. Do you see?"

Obviously she didn't, even when she said she did. What I said wasn't bragging because you don't brag about being insane. What I did made no sense at all. After the old drunk tried to kill me, I kept living with him, eating burnt, starchy cooking, getting punched every once in a while. I could have moved back home. Mom and Dad wanted me to. Doomsday. A cracked ceiling. That was why I didn't move back. But a few months later, I fired the old guy and was back home again … just for a few weeks until I met Moe. I didn't have doomsday hanging over me when I lived at the commune. I could leave at any time … after the scene with Redeye … after the ransacking of my room … after the bomb … after the Chicano attack. I could move back to California, not to live with my folks or even with Jerry … but with Louise on her Hidden garden, swimming nude, staying high, sleeping peacefully under the stained-glass window, waiting for her to sell the place so we could move together back to Santa Fe. But I stayed in the chaos of the commune waiting for Louise to come out ... waiting for two months. Why did I stay in chaos when I could have had the desired peace? I don't know. If I moved back, it would have been admitting defeat inside myself. I had to be right in the middle of things and to be on my own, floating free. The things that were going on around me would have overwhelmed me if I didn't accept everything, working with it and trying to duck the flying chairs and wine bottles. That was what I was trying to show Carol ... that you have got to be idealistic enough to accept people and realistic enough to duck ... to do anything with people. A white woman doesn't walk through a ghetto late at night alone without accepting running into hate ... accepting, not expecting. To still take the walk, to still be free, but also protected by seeing reality!!

"I've been thinking about going back with you. I want to go and be with you for a while." Carol said, driving back to the store, "But I have to be free to go when I have to, be free to do what I want ... to do God's will. Do you understand?"

I grunted sure.

"Mom would worry even more about me than she already does. I just get in her hair, hanging around the house, not doing anything to help, except maybe cooking. She wants me to get a job to meet people and to help support us. But I don't want a job ... I'm quite happy studying about God."

I made a noise to say, oh yeah? Come off of it. "Sitting home, reading books, saying it's not the way it looks, lately, you've been strong, baby, I think you're wrong."

"Well, maybe not happy. If there weren't so many things in the way ... things I'd have to do before we go ... if it weren't for them, I'd go with you right now."

When we were back in the store, with my board back on, I asked, "What sort of things?"

"First, we'd have to buy the car and then wait until my brother sends the title from Germany."

"That's easy. I could give you the money now and we could be off in two weeks. I should have about $135. I don't know exactly how much because Moe would just say that the grass is gone."

"How can you trust me that much? I wouldn't … I don't. How do you know I wouldn't just take the money, buy the car, and then decide I didn't want to go after all? I won't do that. If I took your money and promised you to drive you back, I'd do it no matter what. But how do you know that … how can you be sure?"

"I don't know. Not for sure. But I take risks. If I waited until I was sure, I wouldn't do anything or go anywhere," I said, feeling Moe listening to us as he sat reading about Malcolm X.

"Anyways, my brother wants $200 for the car," Carol said.

Moe dropped the book into his lap and scratched his bushy head. "Excuse me for interrupting your conference, but shithead's math is about as shitty as his spelling. The grass came to $165 … and I think I forgot to tear up the last three checks … they are someplace around."

That mother-fucking Shitface jerkhead sap! I was so proud that I had managed to pay him back, had somehow got ten dollars to him the first thing of every month. Louise had understood how important it was; no matter how tight our family's budget might be … no matter if we ran out of food before the end of the month … the check to D.C. went out. And this asshole didn't cash them! What a dope! And it was impossible that he got that much for ten lids (we smoked the other three up). After I cooled down, I realized that I couldn't stop Moe from being the idiot giver. So the money for the car was out of the way … with a little left for traveling expenses ... not enough to get us there ... but enough to start. Louise would have to send a little more. But Carol still hadn't made up her mind. She would come back tomorrow, maybe with a made-up mind.

CHAPTER XX

The next day was almost like spring.

"What is this?" The businessman with stylish, long sideburns asked, looking down at the board and then up to Moe, who was standing on the tower's steps handing down a package.

"A letter board. He spells out words," Moe said, taking the money.

"How interesting. Are you his trainer?"

"Yes. I trained him by using a Skinners' box. When he pointed to the right letter, I gave him a gumdrop," Moe said.

"It must have taken a long time to train him."

"Ah, yes! Much longer than a pigeon or a mouse would take."

My protesting laugh startled the guy who was studying me with deep interest. "Really, I am his trainer," I said.

The guy went out with his package, not even wondering if Moe had put him on … my line hadn't even reached him.

A group of nine kids came in a little while later with a young man. Not a normal bunch of kids. They acted like the store was a different world than the one they were used to. The young man who seemed to be their teacher had to hold onto the black, eight-year-old to prevent him from fleeing in fright.

"Why do you want to run away?" he asked the young man.

"Donna know … Let's go back to the car … Please, John … Let's go back," said the little boy, and then seeing me, slipped behind John's back to hide. "Donna like that man."

The kids … some of them, went exploring the store, a world of colors, smells, sounds and textures. Most of them ran around staring at the posters and feeling the clothes with the curiosity of kittens. One boy spent his time smelling the scented candles. A blonde-haired kid kept popping questions at Moe about how the motorcycles and blacklights worked and kept asking, "How much?". Two other boys just sat on the car seats withdrawn; the store was a bit too much for them to take it all in.

"Why don't you like him?" John asked, hugging the black boy close to him.

"Donna know. He looks strange. Why is he like that?"

"I don't know. The only way we're going to find out is to ask him," John said, easing the boy towards me. "Can you understand us?"

"Yes," I said.

"Did you see what he does, Jimmy? He spells out words on that board with that thing on his head."

"Why?"

"Because he can't talk."

"Why?"

"When I was born," I said, half-expecting the kid to lose interest before I had finished, "The doctor pulled me out of my mother by my head using something like pliers. He squeezed too hard and cut off oxygen, air, to my brain … the part that controls my movements. So now the message gets scrambled between my hand, say, and my brain…"

The blonde kid got it ... what I was talking about; he was interested in science, even entered a project in the Science Fair. The other boys had crowded around me, listening and watching. Jimmy was still hiding behind John, his eyes wide open.

"Did you sue the doctor?" asked the fat boy standing next to the blonde brain.

"Stupid, you don't sue doctors," said the blonde one.

"If a doctor did that to me, I'd sue him," the fat one said.

"Why should I sue him?" I asked. "He just made a mistake."

They were so interested in me that we talked for a half hour, exchanging names and ages. They asked me questions like why did I slobber. Ralph, the smart kid, asked if I could come visit the school. John liked the idea and said he would come back that night or the next day to talk about it and to get to know me. Carol walked in and stood listening, watching. Jimmy was still huddled behind John, afraid of me.

"Still don't like me?" I asked.

"No."

"I like you," I said.

He didn't come out from behind John, but he knew that I wasn't bullshitting him, that I did really like him. For the first time, he looked me straight in the eye.

After they had gone, Carol asked, "Are those kids mentally retarded?"

"No," answered Moe, "Emotionally disturbed ... which means anything from slow learners to kids who are too smart, too sensitive for their own good. The kids that the world freaks out so bad that they can't function in it ... supposedly. I talked to that guy John ... a good dude ... works with those kids in a special school near here. He brings a bunch of them here every week. This is the only contact they get with the real world, except when they go home for the weekends and get fucked up even more. The school is a weird place, an old mansion. It's supposed to teach the kids how to cope with the world, but it keeps the world from them … and it keeps most of them doped up. If the kid is too speedy, too emotional, too violent, they give him downers; if he is too listless, too slow, they give him something to hype him up. There is even a drug to keep a kid happy. Sure is easier than relating to the kid."

"Could I go when you visit them?" Carol asked me.

"Sure."

CHAPTER XXI

"You better give me the money," Carol told Moe, who was running up the tower steps to change the record. "That's why I came today. Don't ask me why I am doing it, or how I made up my mind. I didn't. But there is nothing I want to do, and Frank does need a ride home."

"Couldn't we just go … send the money and go? Louise will wire me some more," I said. It was getting too complicated, and time has the ability to stretch out while you are taking care of things. I would never have gotten to D.C. in the first place if I'd started thinking how hard the bus ride would be or how dangerous carrying dope was. Other people did that for me … thinking and worrying. Trying to talk sense into me. Sorry, it can't be done.

If I took all of the precautions, then that would be all there would be to do … taking precautions … not doing things, going places. I rarely look realistic. I have dreams, things that I want to do. I believe in dreams. That makes me unrealistic, a dreamer. I've been told that all my life. But I am not satisfied with dreaming, wishing, praying. I take risks to make my dreams into reality. I am a realist in that way. A realist living a dream.

I know things may happen, may attack me. OK. I'll handle them when they do. I can handle them, or someone will be along in a while who can. You never get more than you can handle if you don't freak out and forget that you can handle it. Things will come up. But they can't jump me by surprise because I expect them.

You can be trapped in the fear of things or by the surprise of things. Carol had rational reasons for not going right away. The car had no insurance, so we had to wait until it was transferred into her name so as not to put her brother in risk. That was reasonable, sensible enough ... even though I hadn't planned on getting into wrecks. I was willing to wait for that. With the money left over from the car, Carol was going to the Triple A. You know how cars break down on trips. I didn't know ... but then I was a dreamer who didn't know about things like that, who had forgotten what a dime looked like. There was no money left for gas, oil and food. A call to Louise could get at least $25 more of my welfare money. But Carol wouldn't hear of it. She had already taken more of my money than she should. So, it was up to her to get the extra money ... meaning a job. Right then, my realistic dreamer's sense sensed that it had gotten too complicated, that we should split as soon as possible. But how to go over Carol's morals ... her "should" and "shouldn'ts"? Shouldn't take more money; should help pay for the trip. Then she added one more precaution that she had to take before she could go. Get one other person who was going West to share traveling expenses, to take turns driving, and to help with me on the road. Made rational sense. Especially traveling with me. A girl driving across the country in an old Ford with a crippled guy ... not even money enough to stay in motels. Winter wasn't even over yet. It made perfect sense to get a rider who could take me into the men's rest room in gas stations.

But if I had perfect sense, I'd be home watching TV. But how could I tell her that? So, she went off to mail the money to her brother and to join the Triple A. I kept telling myself that we were going in two weeks. I had to get back soon. Suzy came in a little while later with a bundle of underground newspapers under her arm. It was a good thing she hadn't come in earlier when Carol was there. A comic thought. Suzy might get hurt if she saw me with Carol. There might be a scene if that happened ... if they came in at the same time. Before, I had no girls at all ... and now I had two girls, which was a stickier problem. I began to think how to keep them apart.

I felt like the guy in the control tower when two jets are about to collide. Carol had said she would be back after she joined the Triple A. Which meant ... I slid down in my chair. Oh, no! I looked to Moe for help. He just winked, oh yes! He saw the position I was in and just chuckled. I had to laugh too. Suzy just sat there not being able to figure out what we were laughing at. Although I was laughing, I was afraid. Afraid that if Carol found out that I was, or had been, "involved" with Suzy, she wouldn't take the time to see me. For a minute, I wished Suzy would go away, disappear, shatter. It seems too weird now. Why would what I had with Suzy make any difference to Carol? But that is the layer of dust on a mirror. Dangerous!

I got Suzy to take me selling her papers in front of the drugstore nearby. Got her out of the store. We sold just one paper in the time we spent getting cold in the shadows of sundown ... to a housewife who fumbled in her pocketbook for a quarter and ended up giving us a dollar, almost forgetting to take her paper.

"Would you get jealous if I had another girlfriend?" I felt like a one-year-old asking that in that way, but it cut the fuse.

"No ... do you?"

"Yes. We are going to Santa Fe in a couple of weeks."

"Oh?"

That was all she said about it and went on selling papers as if nothing had happened, as if it didn't affect her. I was happy that she took it so well. I was relaxing into easiness when we got back to the store when Suzy cocked her head, looking at me with sad, lost eyes, and said, "Do you love her more than me?"

"You are jealous!" I tried to laugh but couldn't for a grey feeling inside.

"I am not ... Do you?"

"I can't answer that. I love her in a different way than I love you ... but not more."

Suzy don't get hurt. Don't let me hurt you. Run away. Scream, cry! Hate me. Don't just sit there, lost and helpless. Numb. Don't just be numb. Feel something. You were right ... I can't love somebody that doesn't feel ... not in the way I need to love. Feel, and I wouldn't need to hurt you. You feel ... love, pain, jealousy ... but you won't admit it. You feel unknown.

I don't want to hurt you because I have been hurt in the same way. I knew this pain ... letting myself feel it, everything of it and showed it. I was not a silent martyr. And I knew when the pain stopped because I had felt it and then I had stopped hurting. But Suzy just sat there numbed. She was still sitting there when Carol came in and hugged me.

"The wheels have been set moving. Want to take a ride in our car?"

"Why not," I said.

Suzy kept sitting there, staring at Carol so hard that Carol must have noticed.

"This is Suzy ... the girl I told you about," I said.

"Hi ... Frank, have to talk to Moe before we go," Carol said and walked into the back room.

Suzy didn't speak but started pointing out words on the talking board. Back to the board.

"She is nice. I won't get in your way."

"Good."

"Can I go with you?"

"No. I want to be alone with her," I said as Moe and Carol were coming. Suzy just didn't understand.

Get out of my way, Suzy. Don't stand there in front of me with your sad eyes. I won't accept the wave of guilt that is coming in. Don't follow us outside without your coat ... following us to the car like a shadow. That is all you are. A shadow. A ghost. I can't love a shadow. And I am not afraid of ghosts. So, stop holding the car door, staring at me. I refuse to feel like a bastard ... like I am hurting you. Don't sit in my useless wheelchair, cross legged, like a Buddhist about to be burned.

"Come on, Sexy Suzy. You have a date with me. We'll show them," said Moe, pushing her back to the shop as if she was in a wheelbarrow. We drove away.

The bastard Ford drove away into the night. I wanted to get close to Carol, to lean on her arm, into her, enjoying the ride. But I couldn't. Suzy's face kept staring at me ... the face I might as well have smashed in with a brick. I couldn't listen to Carol's usual monolog or to the radio with its speed talk DJ because everything that Carol was saying, while it had nothing to do with Suzy and me, made it clearer and clearer what I did ... and each song made me more depressed. That was not my usual self ... I didn't go around hurting people. I wanted to go back and talk to her. But it was too late now. I should have become clear as the mirror before we drove away. Suzy might be gone before we got back, or she might stay overnight ... It was hard to tell with her. And I couldn't make up my mind which I was wishing for.

"You haven't been here with me since we left," Carol was saying. "It's like you're thinking way off somewhere ... very solemn, sad. It's that girl, Suzy, isn't it? She wanted something from us, from you. Do you think we should go back to be with her?"

I grunted no. What was the use? "God is a concept by which we measure pain", John Lennon was singing on the radio when she flipped it off. What was the use?

"Good. I didn't want to go back. That girl scared me a little. She doesn't seem quite real … and there was something in her eyes that I didn't understand. But at the same time, I wanted to cuddle her, protect her. She's so tiny, so fragile. You are doing a lot for her just by loving her. Wonder if she believes in Jesus. You should find out. Probably not. That's why she's so lost."

Carol was silent for a while. Without my board, I couldn't tell Carol that Suzy not only believed in Jesus, but she saw him and talked to him.

"Moe slipped me enough grass for a joint," Carol finally said. "Now we need someplace safe to smoke. There is a church up here aways … the world center of Protestant churches. It is one of my favorite places to go and sit. Sometimes. I'll take you when it's open. It has some great stained-glass windows … also, a big empty parking lot."

As we pulled into the driveway past the white church that looked like a bad piece of futuristic art, it started to drizzle. There were just two other cars in the huge parking lot … so the cops couldn't sneak up on us for a surprise attack. Carol rolled a joint and was about to light the coconut incense that Moe had provided in the kit, when we ran into a problem … no match. But Carol wanted to drop by her house to pick up some things that we could use to really celebrate the decision to drive to Santa Fe.

Her house was a large brick house sitting on a hill above the sidewalk. The whole street was sleeping peacefully in the midnight darkness. Carol ran up the steps into the house, leaving me alone in the dark car. It was the first time in weeks that I had been alone … really alone. A thought about Suzy came in … but there would be enough time to worry about that later. I looked at the dark outline of the house. A long way from Before and After. I'd be a flaw in that well of orderliness. After a while, Carol opened the car door, turning on the inside light. She had a match, two cupcakes, and three cans of beer.

"I made these cupcakes this morning and have been saving these beers for when I need to feel good. You do drink don't you?"

"Sometimes. But I like dope better."

"Let's smoke it here … the quiet street is the safest place. Then I want to take you to one of my favorite places."

Carol turned out the car light and lit the joint. Then she put the lighted end in her mouth and blew smoke into my mouth … almost a kiss. The way I had learned to hold my breath since I started smoking dope would have made any speech therapist happy. But it was all show because, except for some super stuff, grass didn't do anything to me. But I always pretended to be stoned because it got people high when they thought they got me high. After the joint was gone, we drove, not saying anything, me leaning on her.

"That is the school that those kids were from today," Carol said as we passed an old stone mansion with a great hilly lawn. "I hadn't noticed it until I drove by today after I left the store. I drive this way but never noticed that it was a school before … kids never play on the lawn. Living there must be like living in a cold castle. All it needs is a moat. I bet the inside looks like a sterile laboratory. Up there ahead is the park … my favorite place. I let Bo off his leash and run with him, pretending not to hear the cars around us. A lot has happened to me here. This is where I first made love a long time ago … up there in the woods."

We turned into a narrow parking lot beside a well-attended green lawn running up the hill to the woods. There was just one other car in the lot … which started up its engine and eased out of it nervously as soon as it saw us approaching. But when it got a better glimpse of us and saw we weren't dangerous, that we were the same as it, it slid into a parking space a little way off from us.

"You can lean on me, but I might have to push you up fast so I can start the car if a cop car comes along. It is illegal to have an open can of beer in the car, you know."

I just couldn't take this paranoia seriously. If we were still smoking a joint, it would have been different. But I couldn't see us getting busted for just drinking beer. Absurd! So, it was just a game to me having to spring up every time a pair of headlights flashed in the rearview mirror, Carol's head turning around, trying to make out what kind of visitor it was, her hand on the key for a quick getaway. The other parked car soon had enough of the game and drove off. But for me, the game just added another bit of excitement to a new experience. I had never parked with a girl alone in the dark, getting drunk before. Carol laid back on the car door and stroked my head on her breast. It was very romantic, except for the piece of cupcake stuck on the roof of my mouth, sticky icing going down my shirt, and beer foaming back out of my mouth and all over everything. I didn't mind. I was enjoying just being like that, close with her.

"Just close your mouth when you've had enough beer. It's been a long time since I came here with guys on dates … just a few dates. That was in high school. Me and a girlfriend would get dressed up, do ourselves up, and go to a bar down in Northeast. Drinking a glass of beer very slowly at a table … we couldn't afford anything else … watching the college guys playing pool … hoping that we weren't too obvious … but also wishing they would notice us. They sometimes did … a few times they brought us up here. That's how I got turned on to grass. Then I let one guy I thought I loved take me here up in the woods. Now you should have seen how I looked then. I was nothing at all how I look now … slim … long hair … wore miniskirts and make-up. I looked so in. But I was so lonely, I wish I had known you then. I tried to make it on my own after high school ... had an apartment of my own and was a secretary. That was the loneliest I ever want to be. I couldn't take it after a few months, so I moved back home and quit the job ... actually, I got fired. I started dropping acid when I had the apartment, and I changed too much so I couldn't stay home for long ... especially after Dad killed himself. Mom used to visit the grave every day, and I went with her. In a way, I like the peace there. I still go there to sit on the grass. I want that peace ... maybe I'll only get it when I die. I think about that a lot when I am driving. Don't worry. It's only a thought. Anyway, I couldn't stay at home after Dad was gone because of the depression there ... the wondering of Mom. So, I hitched out to California ... I did a lot that would shock my friends from church ... things like hopping a freight train and sun-bathing with the hobos on top of the car ... taking my clothes off. I still don't know where that sort of thing is at. How can making love be wrong ... be a sin, when it feels good? I don't know ... I am not sure. I have to do more studying. But it really doesn't matter because I haven't wanted to make love since I was raped here ... in the woods ... when I was walking Bo just a week after I got back from the coast ... and Mom stopped worrying about my safety when I was back under her roof. I didn't tell her about the rape, or about when that Negro attacked me down in Northeast. Why worry her?"

"In a way, I'm glad you can't talk. You just lie there and listen. Sometimes, I get you without your board on purpose. I can't talk to anyone else for very long before they cut me off, interrupt me, stop listening. But you keep listening ... making your noises. Maybe you have no choice ... maybe I'm trapping you. But you really listen ... really understand."

I was just enjoying lying there, feeling her breasts under my head, feeling the warmth being with her ... the three beers that we shared made my body relax ... limply cuddled up against her. This was what I always wanted ... or the start of it at least ... just being with a girl in that warmth without the wheelchair, board and pointer getting in the way. Carol was holding my head, rocking it back and forth. Just watching the rain fall on the windshield, making an ever-changing pattern. Silence. The monolog had stopped.

Everything should have been in a peace. It was close to that. There was a sadness hanging around us. After a little while, Carol pushed me up and started the car to head back to the store. It was about two and D.C. was asleep, with no cars on the streets even though it was a Friday night. For a big city, D.C. went to bed early and bored. But Before and After had another hour to go. Moe's rationalization for the insane weekend hours was that during the summer, the Peking next door had a sidewalk café which would attract buyers into the wee hours. But it was still winter. The real reason for the year round vigil was that the lonely people who rarely bought anything kept trickling in, needing a place to be for a while. Moe waited for them. And he was waiting for us. So was Suzy. I had almost forgotten about her. She came back into my mind when we started back. Again, I kept flipping from wishing she would be gone so I could do whatever was going to happen with Carol that night … flipping to wanting Suzy to still be there so I could talk to her, soften the way. Suzy was there, sitting on Moe's lap.

"Well, I hope you birds had as good a date as me and Sexy Suzy did," Moe said, patting Suzy's knee like Santa Claus. "The best Chinese dinner I've ever ate. And notice her new outfit … She is ready for spring. Her old rags were on the verge of becoming indecent."

"D.C. is a bad influence," I said. "This chick took me to a dark park and got me drunk … well, just a little floating. I'm just an innocent country boy who's gotten drunk only once in my life before."

I wasn't really drunk … only a little hot … and had to piss bad. Moe went back to clear off the mattress, and Carol followed him to go to the throne too. I was alone with Suzy standing in front of me, staring down for a long time. I felt like saying sorry, but didn't … instead, I said, "Don't let me hurt you. I don't want to. Do you believe that?"

"Yes. It's alright. I understand," Suzy pointed out on the board.

The mattress was ready now, and Moe came to carry me back for the piss. As I was pissing, Moe said, "After you left, Suzy was one lonely creature. She started crying. But with my usual amusing tact, I explained to her that you are like me. We can't be tied down to one person … one chick. The time always comes when we have to move on, when things get stale. Love 'em and leave 'em is our motto. But it isn't as heartless as it sounds. It always hurts when it's time to move on, especially when the girl gets it into her pretty head that she wants to marry you and gets hurt because she is trying to hold on to you."

"I went out with a chick from Peru a few months back … a nice kid. But I also was sleeping with a teacher. Both got mad that I was seeing the other one. Carman was supposed to go back to Peru in June. But when the time came, she decided to stay. I had to set her straight … told her that if I was the reason for her staying, she had better go home … and I personally sent her on the plane. But today, I got a letter from her saying she is thinking of coming back … Now I have to write her, waking her up to reality. That is one of the hardest things for me to do. I don't want to hurt her, but I want my freedom. With Debbie, I have an understanding. She knows I sleep with other chicks and she doesn't care … much. Anyway, I showed Suzy that you were like me and she seemed to accept it. Are you done pissing?"

I was and he took the piss can away and zipped me up. I was thankful that Moe explained things to Suzy. Maybe it had been right for me to go with Carol after all. But Moe was wrong. I wasn't like him.

I don't believe in free love … not really … even though I sometimes pretended to myself that I did. I used to believe in it when I was living at home going to college, just reading about things like free love. It sounded like a way to escape the trap of a rigid marriage that my folks had spent their life in … a way not for me, but for other people. I thought that I wouldn't have to worry about such a thing as a marriage trap. But free love sounded like a promise to me. If a girl believed in free love, just maybe, she would be free enough to love me.

When I moved in with Louise, I moved from reading to watching … moved into a hip soap opera. I played the role of advisor, the listener and the watcher … which wasn't a very active role. But I was involved in the emotions and the pains of the usual pattern of a love affair … the beginning, when out of pride, fear or doubt, the two just circle around each other, not being sure what the other is thinking, feeling, wanting. Maybe one takes a retreat, trying to deny the thing, trying to make believe the other one doesn't even exist, at least ugly, not worthy of loving. He comes to me with a thousand reasons why he shouldn't, will not, get involved with her. She comes to me in pain, worry and doubt with stories about how he is ignoring her or worse. I feel everything that both of them feel … even the times when I wished the girl would see me instead. I usually know how a drama will end even in this first act. Then something happens to bring them together. The girl comes to me, her big brother, to tell me of the romantic burst and about life in paradise. I feel this, too. But under this, there are still doubts and fears. I just wait until they come to surface. She comes back to me again, telling me what a bastard he really is, or how she is strangely attracted to some other guy. In a short time, everything is shattered and both are cut, even when they will not admit it, saying they are free again. I could see which ones were just gusts of wind, and which ones could lead to what everyone is looking for … if the two stay together through the shattering … through the feeling trapped.

I saw Louise and Helen going from one affair to another. They would go through cycles from depression to romance to depression again. It was exciting and glamorous living around people like that back in Santa Fe, like living in a romantic novel.

But it was also depressing because I saw how Louise would go into a man looking for someone stronger than she was. She would find someone, but when she started melting into that new strength, she would feel that she was losing a part of herself and felt trapped. Then she would withdraw, usually attacking the guy's strength, making it crumble ... which was not hard to do because she usually got involved with the ones who had one flaw ... She could have healed that flaw if she would stay with it. But when she discovered the flaw, it was after feeling like she had lost herself. The melting into another person. That was what I wanted. I knew it. I wondered why most people don't know that is what they really wanted.

Carol came in from the bathroom and lied down on the floor next to me. After a while, I looked up and saw Suzy standing in the doorway. Like a spirit whom only I could see. Carol, unaware of Suzy, was holding my head in her arms. After standing there for a while, Suzy floated off.

"I am debating whether I should stay here tonight ... sleep on the floor ... or go home," Carol said. "Would it be alright with Moe?"

I grunted yes.

"I don't think I will. I don't feel comfortable here. People might think ... Moe might think that we are going to make love. I don't really care what he thinks ... He has a dirty mind. Maybe I could bring you home overnight sometime. But I can't stay tonight."

When Moe was about to close, Carol got up and slipped out the door. Buzzy had come in and was starting to undress as Moe was turning off the front light. When Moe came back to get me ready for bed, Suzy followed. She just stood in the doorway watching the undressing rites. She was probably going to sleep on the car seats as she always did when she stayed overnight. But no, when Moe covered me with the sheet, she took off her shoes and socks and got under the sheet with me. Moe just smiled knowingly and, turned out the light and wished us a good night.

She was so close to me on the single mattress that I could feel her warmth under her clothes, feel her breath on my bare back. It was like we were riding a motorcycle ... her sitting behind me. I twisted my arm backwards, gently touching her, making sure she was still there. I tried to be gentle. Thought I was. But no matter what I did, I heard the silent ouch! I soon stopped touching her. I didn't want to break the fragile doll.

Suzy was right a long time ago; making love would shatter her ... at least while she was still in her world ... at least with me. I didn't dare to even hug her. I just lay there, enjoying just being with her ... waiting for sleep.

As I waited, I watched the blotches of colors on the screen of vibrating white dots. The blotches were like what you see when the flashbulb goes off or when you turn away from the sun. Except these blotches were different colors. Some were round, like cells seen through a microscope; some looked like long balloons. Some flashed off and on, moving across the screen and some just stayed on, moving across the screen like stars cross the night's sky.

I didn't know what the blotches were. I didn't wonder about them because they always had been there. I saw them even in the day, but I saw them clearer in the darkness. I never told anyone about what I saw because it didn't seem important. But when I was a kid, I called the vibrating white dots atoms or air. People and books said that atoms and air were invisible which meant either I saw what I wasn't supposed to be able to see or I just had picked the wrong word for what I saw.

Now, I was just floating in blackness. The walls and the floor had disappeared, revealing a vast space, perhaps a space without limits. Even with Suzy's body lightly touching mine and with Buzzy lying just a couple of inches from her on the floor, I was absolutely alone. Floating in empty space, I was all that existed. But I felt as if I were falling downward … whichever direction downward was. Falling many millions of miles. Falling down into something unreal. When I landed, it would hurt bad, maybe even kill me. I felt like this when I was a kid. Then I felt so small and alone in the vast blackness, I tried to get my head under the covers, into my own cozy world. But now I just relaxed into the falling. Finally, I went to sleep. When I woke up in the morning, I was in the process of landing. My shoulder had hit the earth, but my legs were still in the air, coming down. I scrambled to grab ahold of something so I wouldn't fall over the cliff behind me. But as I eased back, fearing empty space, I felt Suzy sleeping quietly beside me.

I rolled over onto my back so I could watch her sleeping. In falling, I had kicked off the sheet, useless in the heat of the store. I looked down at my naked body, and then at her, wondering how she looked under her clothes. Slowly, she woke up. At first, there was fear and pain. But soon she remembered where she was and who I was. She relaxed then. For a long while, she just looked at my body, not knowing what to do with it. Please don't think you have to do anything … but please do something with me … love me.

She gingerly put her hand on my chest. It moved up, stroking my face. A cool hand. Then she moved it downward over by body. It was so soothing, but also so frustrating. I wanted to feel something strong, forceful, from her … my body wanted to feel warm pressure. But Suzy could just give me the light cool wind of a ghost.

I wanted to hug her. But I knew that if I so much as touched her, the China doll would shatter. Suzy needed someone who could gently hold her. My body couldn't be that gentle. So, I had to lie there, keeping my arms by my side, just accepting whatever she gave me. Soon she got up and went into the bathroom.

Buzzy opened his eyes and said with a devilish grin, "My, my! All night I was tempted to put my hands on that sweet little ass! They wouldn't believe this if it was in a movie or something. I thought about offering to take Suzy off your hands so you could get it on with Carol … just trying to be helpful. I talked with her for a while after you guys were out. But she was so freaky that I had to go back to Bimbo's to get another drink. She'd take anyone to the funny farm with her … anyone who'd get involved with her. I couldn't touch her with a ten-foot pole … well, maybe just her ass! Probably frigid too."

I stopped Buzzy from saying anything more by rolling off the mattress and onto him, playfully wrestling with him. He cried to Moe that the crippled fag was attacking him. Moe just gave out a grunt from the other side of the wall of shirts. Suzy came out again and looked down at me, her head cocked seriously. I caught hold of her leg under her pants and wouldn't let go until she smiled.

Would anyone hug her gently, warmly … hug her as a woman … bringing her out of her world of painful seriousness? The smile was only the first step. Maybe I could take her onto the next step … making her feel something intensely, deep inside her … either love or hate … make her laugh a gutsy belly laugh or scream … not a weak smile or light rain tears. I couldn't give her what she really needed … someone else had to take over … someone with a gentle body. I would take her where I could … and then? She made a phone call, standing over me, talking in a tone so quiet that I could hardly hear her.

"Is Philip there? OK … Philip? I tried … Please don't hang up … sorry … I was going to meet you last night, but something came up … I know … but I had to stay here … I'm at the store … Could we meet someplace now? Not at the store … please! I will walk to the drugstore three blocks down from here. I will start walking now."

I had goosebumps when she hung up the phone. With one last look at me, she was gone, getting Moe to unlock the door for her. What was she? Some kind of spy?

"They would never believe this if it was a scene in a movie," Buzzy said, getting dressed. "Well, aren't you the writer? Write a film. This could be the love scene. What time is it? Wonder if I could talk someone into taking me to the Ingmar Bergman Festival. Maybe JT. I'll just give him a ring. I dig Bergman's films. Ever see The Seventh Seal? Great, wasn't it? Full of symbolism. It's better than just hanging out … Hello … JT? This is Buzzy. What's happening … Had a party, huh? Wish I had known. A slow night at Bimbos. Who was there? … How about Philip? … No shit? Hep, huh? He has been looking yellow. Guess that blows his medical exam for the Merchant Marines. Wish I'd hear about me. What are you doing today? … How about picking me up at the store and going to see a flick? … Come off it. You know how hard it is hitching in the city in the rain … Fuck you, cheapskate!"

Buzzy slammed down the phone, even though he wasn't really mad, and putting on his brown leather jacket, he walked out into the rain. Moe was getting me dressed when the phone rang.

"Before and After … Hold the line. I will switch you to the owner," Moe said, then putting down the phone quietly, he raced out to the front, up the tower's steps to the other set of phones, caught his breath and calmly said into the phone, "Can I help you? Our accounting department takes care of all our store finances. I would turn you over to our accountant, but unfortunately, he is on a week's vacation. I am sorry that you have been waiting for a month to get paid. How much do we owe … $2,000? Is that all? I am sure Mr. Turners will straighten it out when he returns … Thank you for your patience."

As he finished dressing me, he mumbles, "You'll have to wait your turn … wait until I pay off the other $24,000."

Moe had a hard time maintaining the fiction that the store was making it, especially with all of those bills waiting for us each afternoon. Moe once said he needed to make one hundred every day just to break even. I couldn't see how he could make more than sixty dollars … but then, I wasn't a businessman. Moe wasn't either. He kept the store open on wits alone. I couldn't figure out why he wanted to keep it open … he was fated to be forced to close. But by using his wits, he made an adventure out of his trap … like the exile who decides to rob from the rich and give to the poor. It is more fun that way. The noble bandit is still trapped on the outside of society and will still get caught in the end … but there is something noble about carving a Z on the pompous, smug, Governor's fat ass. Moe was trapped on the sinking ship … but as long as he could outsmart the big clothing manufacturers, making fun at them, he was on top of everything, even when he was going down. John came in that afternoon to get to know me better.

CHAPTER XXII

"The kids kept talking about you all day after we left. They kept asking questions about you … and asking when you could come to the school. Most of them seem to have a very great interest in you … It's almost like people have told them all their lives that they are fucked up … making them be fucked up. And when they see you, they see someone who is supposed to be fucked up like them, but who is really well adjusted. You freaked a couple of kids out … you are a lot for them to take in … Do you mind me saying that?" John asked …

"No."

"Good. It's good to freak them in that way because it gives me an in to them, makes them vulnerable. But the doctors and head teachers got uptight when they saw the kids not behaving according to the theories. When I told the director about you, he was shocked at my 'lack of responsibility' for putting the kids in such a potentially damaging situation. I am just a student in psychology working for my degree … just working there for the experience. He sees me as a foolish upstart. He forbids me to bring you to the school … and I'll get fired if I bring any more kids here … If I get caught, too bad."

"How about if I just show up and talk to the director?" I asked mischievously. I loved to go to places where I was banned.

"A good way to get John canned," Moe observed. "John is needed by the kids there. They need at least one real human."

It would have been fun outraging the stuffed shirts. But unfortunately, Moe was right. The subject changed to my life … how I got my board and pointer … how I went to college and dropped out in my last year … how I was living in a communal family in New Mexico. John became really interested in me, with only a slight trace of professionalism when he learned that not only did I smoke grass, but I had also dropped acid and other drugs that he hadn't dared to experiment with yet.

"Frank is one of the main reasons why I dig drugs, even though I don't take such shit myself. He can't have as many experiences as we can … he can't do things like racing cars or climbing mountains or riding motorcycles. He is very limited in that way. But on acid, he has experiences in his head that are equal to racing cars. And there is an element of risk in his experiences too … the main reason that people race is risking wrecking and dying … to get out of the tight squeezes alive or die a hero. The same with him. That makes life interesting."

CHAPTER XXIII

Moe was right about taking risks. I demanded the right to risk everything that was me or mine. But he was wrong about my being limited in experiences. Why didn't he really know me? Know that I had done everything, that I had experienced almost everything that could be done outwardly …

I had traveled halfway around the world. Attended parties with movie stars. Been in fast-moving racing cars … and in riots. I didn't shoot up smack. I had let other people experience that sort of thing for me while I watched. True, I didn't play basketball … but I didn't want to, as much as the script said I should want to. But I always got to do what I wanted to … in time … always.

I couldn't help laughing inside when someone looked at me in that way, feeling sorry that I couldn't do things. I had done more things than they, had a fuller life. I didn't need to laugh at them … rarely set them straight. I just chuckled inside over the secret.

As a kid, I just couldn't see spending time trying to learn to walk and talk … even when people kept trying to force me into it. I would have liked to talk … that would have set people free with me. But I knew very early that I could never talk, that trying to was just performing useless rites. As for walking, I couldn't see I was missing much by not walking. I wanted to learn, understand, and live much more than I wanted walking and talking. I worked hard at learning, understanding and living because I saw that was the way to real freedom. But people rarely understood that. As for taking acid, Moe was partly right. I did take risks. But the thrill of taking risks was not the reason I took acid. I wanted to get to the other reality so I could see this everyday reality with objectivity, so I could come back into this world with a new perspective … dig this world more.

CHAPTER XXIV

John said he would take me sightseeing on his day off. When he left, he pulled out of his pocket a little yellow snuff tin and slipped it to Moe.

"For Frank … it isn't snuff. It's pretty fair stuff. Hope he gets off."

People always wanted to give me things … candy, ice cream, dope, money. After John left, I set to work finding a rider for the trip … looking through the want ads in the underground paper. There was someone wanting a ride to Dallas … which would have been ideal … Carol and I would make it from Texas to Santa Fe alone easy. There was someone else who was willing to "go with anyone anywhere." Not what we were looking for exactly. There was an ad from a handicapped nineteen-year-old who wanted "to meet a chick." Sounded familiar.

I just had to wait until a rider came in. One did. An acid ghost named Jim … glassy, blown-out eyes, dreamily talking, in slow motion, the fatality of physically fried brain cells. It took forever to track down the word he wanted to say … forever to decide if he would eat the hamburger that he held. He usually just hung around the store, sometimes helping Moe by neatly stacking up bellbottoms … or answering the phone … or turning over the record. Anything to feel useful. He hadn't been in the last two weeks because he got a job at a shoe store. He had hoped to get enough money to get his trumpet out of hock.

"I think I'm going to get fired soon … or quit. But I won't have enough to get my horn back," he said as if he was talking in his sleep, staring into space. "I can't take their hassling me, hurrying me to do this, do that … I get lost, blank out. My head can't handle it. I'm not a salesman. I am a musician. But when will bands start using horns again?"

"The two bands in Santa Fe are starting to experiment with horns," I said.

After he fitted the puzzle of letters and words finally together in the right order in his head … it took my spelling the line over three times before that happened … Jim's face woke up. "Really? Do you think they need a good trumpet?"

I went into my Santa Fe spiel, emphasizing the coffeehouse that the two bands own and run together … telling him there was a loose group of musicians that he would fit into. He wanted to go, wanted to be our rider. He could hang on at the job for another two weeks to get the money for his contribution to the trip … but not for the two months needed to ransom the horn. However, he couldn't' make his mind up. It swirled around in him, making him dizzy. What good was a horn player without his horn? Although Jim wasn't happy here in D.C., he could survive here … he knew the ropes, the tricks. How could he be sure he could survive there, even though it was heaven? He said he would make up his mind and would come back. I had a feeling that Jim could never make up his mind and the next time, he would still be in the fog. When Carol came in later that day, I told her about Jim.

"But I don't think we should count on him," I said. "How about calling that rider going to Texas … and calling the Switchboard so they will put us on their rides board?"

"I've been thinking today. I don't want just any rider. I want to travel with a real Christian," Carol said in a hard tone that pushed me backwards away from her. "Someone that won't let me stray from the path. I'm weak ... I give in to temptations too easy. Like last night."

"What about last night? Oh!" I had a flash of understanding. "You did what you know that you shouldn't do ... drinking beer, smoking dope ... maybe even smoking cigarettes."

"That's partly it. I escape into those things when I can't stand the pain any more ... Rather than going through the trials that Jesus sets before me ... the fires that would strengthen me, harden me. Instead, every time, I fall into the temptations that Satan has set right in front of me. Temptation of going off and hiding ... lighting up a cigarette when I get nervous ... like right now," Carol said, crushing the cigarette out on the floor violently. "Why am I so weak! Whenever the loneliness and pain get to be too much for me to stand, I get stoned or drunk ... or eat ... instead of calling on the Lord to lift me up. Maybe I don't really believe that He will pick me up when I've had enough."

She knew so much of why she did things, how she avoided looking at her pain and loneliness and avoided really doing something about it. No. That isn't right. Carol didn't know or see. Something inside of her knew and saw ... and was trying to get the truth out. But Carol didn't hear the truth that she spoke. People rarely did. Talking to her was like listening to a person with a knowing and talking to an ignorant person at the same time.

"What we did last night was good ... more than good. It was something I have waited for for a long time ... The same thing happened on the mattress that time," I said.

"What's that?"

"We loved each other."

"Loved just to get away from the pain and loneliness. I loved for the same reason why I get stoned ... to hide from the pain."

"Stop feeling guilty about what you do!" I jabbed on the board. I didn't care whether or not we drank or smoked the joint last night. It didn't matter. It felt good ... the smoking and drinking felt good because we loved each other ... we loved each other. That's what's real. Don't be blind to that by being guilty ... by feeling guilty!

"This is why I want another real Christian traveling with me ... with us, I mean. To keep me from getting confused."

"By who?"

"By you. You are confusing me right now."

"How can I, if you really believe what you think you believe ... if it is true?"

Carol was quiet for a while. Moe was sitting on the car seats, talking to Wattbulb, a tall, black social worker, about our new unofficial sale.

"Yeah, half off on everything ... well, just clothes," Moe said with his book on Malcolm X in his lap. "Offer is good for blacks only. If you're white, you're out of luck."

"Aren't you afraid of being charged with reverse racism?" Wattbulb asked in a deep, cultured voice.

"No. I don't have the money to advertise it. So I just tell every black to divide by two what is on the tag. So, the whites don't know about it. But the news will get around in the black community fast. Anyhow, race isn't really the reason. Blacks just buy the clothes that they really want when they finally get enough money. They buy the clothes that I like ... flashy ... wild ... pants with huge elephant bells. Even if I go out of business, I refuse to sell the sissy flairs the whites want to buy ... think they should buy. The whites limit themselves by what they think is safe to wear ... what they should wear. The way I see it, if they want to be safe, they'll have to pay for it."

Their conversation turned to politics and the latest injustices laid on the poor people. It was interesting to them, because Wattbulb had a clear understanding of the problems involved and had some new inside scoops, not clouded by emotion, of what new trickery the government was trying to pull. Interesting to my journalistic reformer's mind because Wattbulb showed some new side of the problems. He didn't have any answers, any solutions, he didn't pretend to. He just spent his days trying to make things a little easier for the people until the answer was found. While they were talking, Carol went over to sit next to them, leaving me nine feet from them. All of a sudden, she interrupted them to attack Wattbulb for seeing everything material and seeking the answers in the world of politics and violence … in the world of man … when all of the answers were within God through Jesus.

"When will Man learn that the only way he can ever change the world is individually changing himself inwardly, getting back to God? Getting back like he was before Adam and Eve sinned," Carol said, busy thinking what to say next, how to teach Wattbulb something. "Man shouldn't concern himself with government. Let the men who are in government govern … they are doing a fair job, all things considered. We should just concern ourselves with finding out what God's will is and following it."

Wattbulb just listened to all of this patiently and then said, "I really do believe in God. But we live in this material world, and we have to use what is around us in this world. I have a baby to feed and protect from the rats. I wouldn't be doing that if I sat in my room meditating on God."

"Man does not live by bread alone."

It went on and on like this for a half hour at least. Wattbulb gently tried to bring Carol down to earth with calm reasoning. But Carol got more wound up, thinking he was denying her Lord, getting more frustrated at not being able to bring him into the light. I just sat there uninvolved, listening to them, wondering what had made her suddenly rigid. I knew the needs of a fanatic were always in her. But what set them free? Guilt? Doubt. Fear. Finally, she had become so obnoxious that she had pushed Wattbulb into a place where he could either try to push her back into her own absurdity or walk away. He chose walking out of the store. She tried to continue the debate with Moe. But Moe just laughed at her, refusing to take her seriously. So, she came back to me.

"Jesus said it would be lonely being a true Christian. Everyone will deny me like they did," Carol said. "Why don't you believe in Jesus?"

"What makes you think I don't?"

"Because you never talk about Him. You've never gone out on a limb and declared your faith to me."

"How dare you! Being so arrogant! Why should I have to confess my faith to you?" My indignity, the force behind it, surprised me even more than it did Carol. I felt I had to soften it by adding, "Besides, you never asked."

"Well, I am asking you now. I have to know because I cannot … will not … be close to anyone who isn't a true Christian. Are you a Christian? Do you believe in Jesus Christ? Not just in God, but in Jesus as your personal savior?"

"If I said I did, what would that prove?"

"It'd prove to me that you are willing to go out on a limb, to risk shame for Jesus."

"I don't have to prove anything to you. I can't! I won't!" I poked out on the board, then went on sadly, "Words do not prove anything. What you feel from me does even more than what I do. What do you feel from me?"

"I feel a peace and a great deal of love ... that is why I want to be around you. You also have more knowledge than I have. I'm a little afraid of that because you could twist your knowledge and use it to confuse me, to lead me from Jesus."

"I don't really feel peace all the time ... I don't think I do ... It rarely feels like it to me. And I don't know how much real knowledge I've got ... I do know things. But that isn't real knowledge. I want wisdom. But what I do have is love. I hope you can feel it from me because I can't prove it any other way than the feeling."

"I do feel it."

"That love makes me a Christian ... I think."

"No, it doesn't. I'm not sure with you because I feel such a powerful thing from you. How can you be a true Christian if I feel you trying to argue against Jesus through me? Or you are just on the verge of giving your life to Jesus. Most people say they believe in God and love ... maybe they even really do. But they have not been saved because they haven't made the commitment to Christ. They may do good things all their lives, but they won't get into the Kingdom of God. It's faith that gets you there, not what you do. Most people who go to Church on Sunday aren't even Christians because they won't dare to look like an asshole for Christ. That is my greatest trial ... to swallow my pride and look like a fool to spread the word. That's why I failed with that Negro ... Wattbulb or whatever his name was ... I failed because I got overawed by his worldly knowledge, by his facts of earth. I withdrew a slight bit from Jesus and the Bible rather than standing firm in them. I got pushed back."

"That isn't why you didn't get through to him," I said, knowing that I didn't want to be around when Carol stood "firm" ... rigid ... on what she thought were the Bible and Jesus.

"Why didn't I then?"

"Because you didn't take the time to love Wattbulb, to get to know him, to listen to him … really listen to him … Am I listening to you … really listening with you? Of course, I am not agreeing with everything you say. But am I openly listening to you, not closing you out as Wattbulb finally did?"

"Yes. You are very open to receiving the Word … even though you haven't fully accepted it yet."

"It has got nothing to do with me. If you had hit me with the "Word" cold, I probably wouldn't have been as gentle as Wattbulb. But you did something to me, with me, before you opened your truths to me."

"I wasn't totally committed to Jesus until I had a revelation last night."

"Do you know what you did to make me want to listen to you? You made friends with me. You let yourself love me and made me love you … in the car last night and on the mattress that night when you gave me the massage. Now that I am something more to you than a mere soul that you want to save, but not to know … and now that you're something more to me than just a Jesus freak trying to lay her trip on me … now I can listen when you open up your ideas."

"If you don't stop confusing us, I will have to leave," Carol said, fear in her eyes.

"But I'm not trying to confuse you … or make you change what you believe."

"Even if you aren't trying, you're doing a good job … of confusing me … not of changing my belief in the Lord."

"I'm just trying to show you a better way to do what you want to … what you want, not what I want. You want to bring people to

Christ. Right? What I'm saying is you can save people easier by giving them a part of you … by taking a part of them in return … rather than giving them just pious words. Words won't save or convert … but what you are naturally will change people, if you let it … if you let what you are shine."

"I have to go before I let you lead me into false pride, the unforgivable sin against God. You're telling me I can do something without Jesus, without using His Word – the Bible, without letting Him come through me and guide me in everything I do. Something inside wants to listen and believe you. But it's just my rebellious pride that would take me away from Jesus. Every time I listen to that, I get fucked up and Jesus has to come and rescue me. That is why I have to leave now … to not listen to my pride coming through you and fall into temptation," Carol said, getting up to leave. But she stopped, shaking her head sadly, "Why am I so weak?"

"Would you believe I am a Christian?" I asked solemnly.

"I would," Carol said, and walked out the door without looking at me.

I hope that Moe didn't overhear my last question. What was I doing implying that I was really a real Christian? I was as much a Christian as Moe. The last time I was even close to a straight church was a high school youth fellowship class near my folks' house four years ago. All the "in" kids of the high school … honor students, football players, homecoming queens, school politicians … belonged to this church. We sat in a circle hearing about a black church that had been burnt down. There were many fine speeches about how we should lift up our less fortunate brothers. The plate was passed around to start this project moving. The plate made it around without stopping even once and returned to the leader's hands as empty as it started. The leader's "Come on, you guys!" didn't help and he wisely let the project fade away. After the meeting, the cigarette machine did a booming business as the kids chattered plans for a beach party next week. I never went back ... like I never went back to Vacation Bible School when I was ten, after the whole class ganged up on this one girl who they thought was always "acting naughty", whatever that meant. Finally, she ran out of the room, crying, having trouble opening the door. After she left, the class went back to studying about the Tower of Babel as if nothing had happened. I sat there too ... trapped. I wanted to go out to comfort the girl, letting her know there was someone who understood, who saw her ... saw her wild, but not as a naughty spirit. I didn't know her at all, only watched her a few times, observing her like I would watch an actor on TV. Once in a while, she would look my way and flash a warm smile. That was all that there was between us. She was only the match that made me start seeing what the Christian Church was. I didn't have the talking board until years after. So I had to ...

[*Editor's Note:* This is where the document ends.]

Mirror of Before & After
a film proposal

INTRODUCTION

MIRROR OF BEFORE AND AFTER will be a one-hundred-minute, color, thirty-five-millimeter, feature film.

The main character is Frank, a twenty-six-year-old man with cerebral palsy who sits in his wheelchair in a head shop in Washington, D.C. trying to communicate with people by pointing out words printed on a board, using a pointer strapped to his head.

The film describes his relationships with Suzy, Carol and Moe. Suzy, who has escaped from a mental hospital, shares with Frank the secrets and voices that guide her mystical and isolated reality. Carol brings Frank out for rides and movies and into his first physical closeness, but later she withdraws into the Jesus Freak movement and tries to heal him instead of love him. Moe, a bushy haired giant, runs the "Before and After" headshop, and has been Frank's friend for many years. Frank tries to draw Moe out of his secret loneliness, coaxing him, questioning him, pulling him from the glittering trap the "Before and After" has become. Frank acts as a mirror for the audience, revealing these three friends clearly.

The film is aimed at the general audience. Its cinematic style is realistic, except for an entrance into Frank and Suzy's inner world which is surreal.

SUMMARY

At the beginning, we follow a seven-year-old black boy as he enters into the headshop and looks at the posters, Zap, hash pipes, etc., soaking up the world of the shop where teenage girls are teasing pimple faced boys and where older boys are sneaking a look at a girl in the dressing room. In the middle of this, he stares at Frank, sitting in the corner. Then he goes back to his browsing, lighting up a cigarette.

Moe is talking to Frank. (Frank communicates by pointing with a wooden stick strapped to his forehead, pointing to letters on a lapboard.) Suzy enters the store like a sad, silent ghost and sits near them, listening. After Moe leaves, Frank becomes aware of her and tries to start a conversation. (The words which are spelled out on a board are shown on subtitles.) He makes out that she is not able to utter a sound. He gets her to use his board and tries unsuccessfully to get her to talk about herself, except to say that she wants to leave this "world that shatters you." We enter a flash of his dream image of her, then we drop back into reality. He reaches for her hand, and reaches into her world, triggering a smile from her, which frightens her. She runs out of the store.

Her next visit gives us and Frank more information about her, but not of her name or the past. Again, we enter Frank's inner world of imagination. When reality returns, Suzy has fallen asleep. When she wakes up, she is lost in fear. She tries to rush out of the store, but she is dizzy. Moe grabs her and tries to talk some sense into her in his rough, satanic way, but he ends up driving her home. "Home" is an empty street. Moe and Frank are left with the unsettling feeling that she doesn't live anywhere.

As Frank wonders for days about Suzy, worrying whether she will come again, we begin to see Moe's almost maternal relationship with Frank.

But Suzy does come back. This time she starts revealing her private, inner world to Frank, telling him she hears voices and met Jesus yesterday. We enter her nightmare world, seeing her with Jesus. Jesus says she will shatter soon. Back to reality, Frank pleads with her not to die, because he loves and needs her. She says he can't love her because she is not real. We learn that Frank is just in D.C. for a visit and is going back to California where he goes to college and has an apartment with his brother. Suzy is startled by Frank's plans to leave and says, "This is why I don't like your world."

During Suzy's next visit, Frank asks, "Will you make love with me?" Again, we go into Frank's mind where sexual, almost violent, images are flashing. We also learn that Suzy is absolutely afraid of sex. Frank drops his demand.

During her last visit before Frank leaves, he asks her to come with him to California. But something she calls, "The Curse", stands in the way, even when she says she wants to come. Frank gropes for some kind of understanding of "The Curse" and of her saying she doesn't exist, searching for something with which to break "The Curse." Moe offers to pay Suzy's airfare. But Suzy cannot give a definite answer because she has to do something first and cannot make promises because she does not exist.

But she starts telling him of her past, how her parents tried to kill her on their West Virginia farm, how she lost her voice because off shock, how she ran away to New York City, and how the police picked her up, and when she couldn't speak and wouldn't give her name, they put her in a mental hospital and called her Suzy, and finally, how she escaped. She says she has to help her friend escape before she can go West. Frank tries unsuccessfully to talk her out of this. She still doesn't promise him she will come. But she laughs, the first sound she has made throughout the film. It is a sign to Frank that he can go without worry about her, because in some way he has broken through to her.

He returns to California to an unexpected hostile reaction. The prospect of Suzy's coming to live with Frank threatens his brother who is getting money for taking care of Frank. And more importantly, his brother needs this job as a way to get out from under the parental roof. Both his brother and his mother attack Frank for his "unrealistic" hope that Suzy will come. His mother's own feelings of inferiority and her protective attitude toward Frank are shown in lines such as, "How many times do you have to be crushed before you will stop letting yourself be hurt?" and "Any girl that would want you must be sick." Frank feels completely estranged from his family, but this kind of estrangement marks a new beginning for Frank's life and for the film.

The film flashes forward in time. We see Frank locked inside a bus station pay toilet with a nice, meek looking young man, trying to get him out. After Frank is rescued, they go outside to, as we learn, wait for Moe to pick them up. We learn from their conversation that during the year between the present and the last time we saw Frank, he has dropped out of college, cut ties with his family; and he has hitched to Santa Fe, New Mexico, at first to live at a hippy crash pad, and now he is living a seemingly pleasant life in a small communal family. He is just on a Christmas visit to D.C. and to Moe. Dennis, the nice young man, who traveled with Frank on the bus, tells of his plans. But his plans suddenly change after Moe arrives and putting Frank into the car, asks Frank how much Marijuana he is carrying.

At the shop, Frank gets Moe alone to tell him he thinks Dennis is an FBI agent. We cut to the next day. After dusting in the store, Dennis leaves for a few minutes, and Frank gets busy hustling to get the local dealers who hang around the store to sell his grass for him. Frank explains why he had to travel with an FBI agent. As the dealer goes into the bathroom to test the grass, Dennis comes back with two of his "Cuzins" to meet his "Friends". After they browse, they leave. Dennis follows them, after making a call for a "Job". The dope dealer comes out of the john, stoned, and Moe makes a character analysis of Dennis.

Now it is early evening. Moe feeds Frank while talking to his girl, Debbie. Dennis is still dusting. He goes into the backroom where Frank's bag is. Frank happens to look into the backroom to see Dennis going through his bag. Frank continues eating. When Dennis goes out, Frank tells Moe, and Moe has Debbie take the dope out of the shop. Dennis returns and very soon after, four cops come in. Moe invites them to browse. After the cops leave, empty-handed, Dennis decides he will visit his "Relative in West Virginia".

We cut to a day when Moe is feeding Frank and at the same time, refereeing a fight between a high school boy and his Jewish father, who is trying to use an American Flag fringe jacket as a bribe for the completion of his son's term paper. The son wins. The fourth major character comes into both the store and the film for the first time. At first we aren't sure whether it is a boy or a girl. But, when Moe is off waiting on a customer, and the character asks Frank if he wants to be fed, we are sure Carol is a girl. Frank starts talking to her. We find out that Carol is leading a boring existence in the city. She asks Frank if he needs a friend. She promises she will come back and take him out for rides. After she leaves, Frank just sits. We enter his daydream world in which he is a Rock superstar giving a concert, ending a song, and then telling his audience how he and his band have come from another world to do a mission. Frank is brought out of his daydream world by Moe, pouring orange juice into his mouth. An old woman comes in. She takes one look at Frank and starts giving Moe a lecture on how proper vitamins and a hairbrush would heal Frank. Both Frank and Moe defend themselves with sarcasm.

Cut to Frank and Carol talking in the store about why Frank can't fly alone. Because of airline rules, he needs to find some other way back to Santa Fe. Carol tells him about her brother's car that is for sale. Frank says he will buy the car for her with the money he has gotten for his grass if she will drive him to Santa Fe. She isn't sure. He tells her about his philosophy about taking risks. She leaves the store, thinking about his proposal.

Debbie, Moe's girlfriend, walks up to feed Frank and to talk to him about how she can get closer to Moe. We once again enter Frank's inner world. We see, at first Frank and then Moe, lying in bed in a dark room, totally dependent upon other people. Frank tells her that Moe has to learn "The Art of Receiving", and that she should disguise her love more sneakily, so that Moe has to accept it.

Buzy, a Black who hangs around the shop, comes in to ask Moe to get his father to pull some strings to get Buzy into the Merchant Marine School. As Moe closes down the store, and lies Frank down for the night, the conversation turns to Moe's parents, revealing Moe's deep hate for his Mother and his intense, sad love for his Father. As the lights go off, Frank is on a mattress in the Backroom with Buzy going to sleep on the floor beside him. Moe and Debbie make love on the floor in the front of the store.

During the night, we see Debbie walking, nude, through the backroom to the bathroom. We cut to a close-up of Frank's face, awake, watching her, revealing his loneliness and desire.

It is morning, and we see Moe's morning ritual of opening the store, and dressing Frank. There is a phone call from Suzy. Hard cut to her face through the front window, a healthier face. She comes in to talk to Frank, not on the board, but actually with her voice. We learn that Suzy didn't fly to be with Frank in California because "you were with me in my world". They go for a walk outside; but they don't get very far before it becomes clear that she still travels with invisible spirits and still is caught in useless inner rituals. The walk is a battle between Frank's real world and Suzy's surreal world.

Back in the shop, Frank gets Suzy to tell him her invisible friend's name, "Past". Suzy tries to leave but gets trapped in her ritual of going through doors many times. Debbie and Frank watch her as she finally gets through the door. Then, they talk about her.

Frank and Carol walk out of a library and stop to talk for a while. She invites him for a ride tomorrow, with some marijuana. Then she starts telling him, using the shop as a symbol for the material world, how the world keeps closing in on her with its "Corruption and Temptation".

We now see them in the car, driving. Frank is lying with his head in her lap. She strokes his body with her free hand as she rambles in a monolog. We learn more about Carol; about how she hated her very "Religious" Father, who hit her, how she feels guilty about having felt nothing but relief when she found him dead after he shot himself.

Outside the shop, Moe carries Frank playfully into the shop where Carol is waiting to take his clothes off and to give him a massage. We start having daydream flashes, in between reality, flashes of their making love, Throughout the scene, her monolog continues, in which she tells Frank that her weak part feels love, acceptance and the simple feeling of being comfortable; but she mustn't give in to these feelings. She must be spiritually strong. Reality fades into the daydream of lovemaking. When we return to reality again, Moe, not Carol, is dressing him.

Moe and Frank talk about how hard it is to get girls out of D.C.

Once again Carol and Frank are in the car. Carol is in her monolog again. We learn that she had left yesterday because she started feeling a human melting love for Frank. But, although she'd left, "She was still with him in spirit". Frank winces. She tells him how purely spiritual he is. He winces again.

They are parked. Frank has his board. Carol asks him how he, being spiritual, can live in the stronghold of materiality and sin. She can't without being influenced, without being just like "Them".

Frank tells her of his philosophy of seeing things for what they are, enjoying what is good in everything and learning from what is bad. Carol starts telling him about the events that have made her scared of people. She lets Jesus love people for her. Frank tells her of the times when people have tried to kill him; but this did not crush him or make him pull back from people, because he has seen what people really are like and has learned to duck the evil. They start talking about the trip to Santa Fe.

Frank and Moe are sitting in the store. A businessman comes in and stares at Frank. Moe and Frank artfully put him down. He leaves, unaware that he has been put down. Carol comes in and asks Moe for Frank's grass money, to buy her brother's car. She has decided to make the trip, but she has to wait for two more weeks. Frank unsuccessfully tries to get her to leave right away.

Frank and Suzy are selling underground newspapers on the street. Frank tells her about Carol and their plans. She is hurt. He feels guilty.

Suzy and Frank are sitting in the store. Carol comes in and hugs Frank but goes back to talk to Moe. Suzy uses the board to tell Frank she won't get in his way with Carol but asks him if she can come for the ride. He flatly says no. She follows Frank, Carol and Moe out to the car. After Moe puts Frank into the car, he gently picks up Suzy and puts her in the wheelchair to roll her back inside the store. As Frank and Carol drive, he tries to cozy up to her, but Suzy's sad face keeps flashing before him. Carol senses Frank's preoccupation but Frank refuses to go back to the shop. Carol says she is frightened of Suzy, as she would be of a ghost, but that she sees how much good Frank is doing for Suzy.

They are parked in the empty parking lot of a park, smoking pot, drinking beer, eating cupcakes. Frank, his beard gooey with beer foam and cake icing, lies on the seat with his head in Carol's lap, listening to how she made love in this park for the first time. She blows pot smoke into his mouth, almost kissing him, but the undercurrent of paranoia surfaces whenever a car drives by. Carol goes into a monologue in which she tells Frank about the lonely time in High School, about hanging around in bars, waiting to be picked up, about the short time of lonely independence, about her hippy life in California, about her return to D.C. in disgrace. This scene is a series of long takes of Frank quietly listening to her and of quick flashes of his fantasy of their making love.

Suzy and Moe are sitting together in the shop. She is crying, as Moe is trying, in his ironic way, to explain Frank's actions, but in terms of free love. Suzy is wearing a new outfit that Moe has just given her. Frank and Carol enter. After a little joking, Moe and Carol leave Frank and Suzy alone. Frank tries to explain that he doesn't want to hurt her. She says that she understands and is trying to understand free love. Frank says he doesn't believe in free love. He has known too many hippies for him to believe that free love leads to happiness. He tries to explain that she can't give him what he needs, a full, committed, male-female relationship, if she is in her own private world. Carol can give him this. Carol comes over to talk to Frank and Suzy withdraws into a corner. Carol says she wants to sleep with him tonight but then chickens out and leaves. Moe undresses Frank for bed. Suzy watches. When Frank is under the covers, she only takes off her shoes and socks and gets under the covers with him. We watch them as the covers are kicked off, watching her as she unsuccessfully tries to find her way into the strange, frightening world of sex, by stroking his nude body, too timidly, too lightly. He tries to stroke her, but every time he touches her, she pulls away in pain.

Frank is talking to Buzy about the frustrating experience, saying she is too fragile for him. Buzy jokingly says even he is attracted to Suzy, but he would never touch her because she is so looney that she would probably make him looney too. Frank starts suggesting that Buzy should go after Suzy. That would solve Frank's problem with his conscience.

Carol and Frank are sitting in a park talking. She says they can't leave on their trip until they find another rider to go with them. But she cuts him off when he starts discussing ways of finding one, to tell him that this rider must be a "Christian" who would keep her from getting weak and falling into temptation like she did last night. Frank tries to make her see that she did what was good last night because she was just being a loving human. But then she cuts off, almost completely, because she thinks he is trying to tempt and confuse her.

Frank is sitting in the shop with Moe, telling him how worried he feels, because Carol hasn't come in for a week. Carol comes in ecstatically gleaming. She says she has been fasting and praying for an answer concerning them. She takes Frank out for a ride.

They are parked in the roadside park beside the river. She reads a prayer from her new book, while hugging him tightly. Then they get out and start walking beside the river. She tells him of a strange prayer meeting that she went to yesterday, where people went into a trancelike state to pray in unknown languages and to get messages directly from Jesus. Frank listens to this with an open mind, but with also a dread of what is coming. We learn that Carol has asked them about Frank. The answer came back from Jesus that Carol is Jesus's agent working on Frank, and that she is the instrument who will be the healing channel and the guide for his salvation. At this point, Frank explodes in sad anger. Why doesn't she see him? Why doesn't she see what he has to do with people through the tool that Jesus has already given him in the form of his body? She says he is just comfortable in his present condition and is putting all of these rationalizations up so he won't have to face the responsibilities that he would have if he were healed. They walk back to the car in silence. Night has fallen as they have been talking, and the streetlights are on. She kneels in front of him, beside the car to pray very passionately. She prays that he will be healed so she can love him in a woman's way. He is crying. She picks up Frank and holds him high above her for a long time, enjoying the new strength that Jesus has given her. As she puts him into the car, she accidentally breaks his pointer. He gets her to give him his board again. He tells her he will try her way completely with an open mind if she will try his way. We see them driving fast and wild, as she drives, she holds him close to her as she would a lover.

We see Frank in the front seat of a flashy new car sitting between Carol and Mike, a balding young man with glasses and a suit. As the scene goes on it becomes clear that Frank wants to curl up and melt into Carol just to get away from this Mike. After Carol and Mike sing a Jesus song, we learn that he is the leader of the prayer group. Mike tries to comfort Frank by telling him to accept the strange things which are about to happen as natural and that the couple whose house is being used for the meeting would accept him into their hearts just fine. But Frank becomes increasingly upset. Mike asks Carol about her relationship to Frank. She tells him how she "discovered Frank in one of those headshops" and how she might drive him to Santa Fe, but perhaps she would stay in DC to do God's work. Frank drops into sad shock.

Frank and Carol are in the middle of a circle in an upper middle-class house. In the circle there is an old woman, a young old maid and a milk toast couple. They are telling Carol who is kneeling beside Frank how nice she is to take on the responsibility of Frank. But Mike warns her about letting personal human feeling get in the way of God's will. Now the people start slowly rocking, singing or chanting each in their own way. This reaches a peak of intensity, then is cut off by Mike standing up and reading a scripture that he says comes directly from God to Frank. He leaves the room as people build the intensity again. The individual songs and chants merge into one piece of intensity which is counter-pointed by the over voice of Mike in the next room, preaching, on the phone, fire and damnation, to a girl in the hospital, paralyzed from a motorcycle accident the day before. The intensity makes the people get up and move almost sexually stroking Frank and Carol. Carol is in an ecstatic state, half crying, half laughing, hugging and kissing Frank. Frank joins in, letting himself melt into the flowing intensity.

Frank is sitting with Mike in the car in front of the store. Carol comes out carrying a change of clothes for Frank. As she climbs in, she says that Suzy just asked her if she could go with them to Santa Fe.

Frank is lying on a mattress in a well-polished bedroom watching Carol undressing. She puts on PJ bottoms. She comes to Frank, puts her arms around him and presses him to her bare breasts. She tells him she feels now spiritually married to him in Jesus, but not physically married to him. She cuts off when they reach a certain physical intensity and lies down on her separate mat beside Frank's to sleep.

Carol is giving Frank a bath.

Carol is fixing breakfast, talking about getting a job for traveling money. Frank sees it as another delay, but Carol insists, looks through the want ads, calls and makes an appointment for an interview. She then gets made up and dressed up. She gives Frank a present: a Bible.

We see Frank reading the Bible in the shop. Buzy accuses him, half-jokingly, of becoming religious to make Carol. Frank says he is getting answers by reading, but not the answers Carol wants him to get. Frank talks about feeling a strange restlessness, about his getting insights that have no apparent link to what he is reading but are triggered off while he is reading. Buzy changes the subject and tells how Suzy slapped him when he made a pass at her last night.

Frank still reads the Bible. Suzy comes in. She is shocked when Frank tells her he slept at Carols' house last night. She starts crying. Frank screams at her, trying to make her feel something intensely, intense enough to explode her private world of illness, to bring her out where she can give him what he needs. Either love me or hate me, either make love with me or kill me. This is what Frank screams on his board. He tries to pressure her into killing him for her to feel something. But he suddenly becomes quiet when it doesn't work. When she says Jesus has told her to go back to the mental hospital because their world is getting too cold for her, Frank agrees with her.

Frank is sitting in the store. A guy with an electric mandolin comes in and starts talking to Frank about God. Then he asks Moe if he could sleep in the shop. Moe starts undressing Frank. The guy comes up and accuses Frank of being an actor who puts everyone on. Frank just grins. But the guy grows violent and says he doesn't like his mind to be played with by a parasite like Frank who wants to live his life sucking off people. He says he knows Frank can really talk. He walks toward Frank saying if Frank doesn't stop screaming and start talking, he will choke him to death. Moe steps in the way.

Carol and Frank are driving, and she tells him about her bad luck job-hunting. They stop at a drive-in hamburger joint where she gets mistaken for a boy. As they eat, she says she really wants to be ugly because then she would have less temptation.

They are in a church looking at a stained-glass window depicting the men who have helped mankind, some of them weren't Christians. Frank starts talking about what he has been thinking about. He says although the prayer meeting moved him, that sort of thing isn't for him, nor is going around overtly trying to convert people. But he has to be where people are, helping people, quietly preparing the way for people to discover Christ in their own way. He says he has seen that he can't cop out on that as he has been doing in Santa Fe. But he can only do this if Carol will share this with him. She says she wants to hide away from people, hide in Christian fellowship, hide until her faith is strong enough to drag people to Christ. Frank just says it sounds as if she has put limits on what she will do for Jesus because the quiet living of Jesus' teachings in the world is harder than either hiding or making a grand show of believing. He asks her just to pray about it. He wants to spend the night reading John together. But Carol is going to a prayer meeting. If Frank wants to be with her, he will have to go to the meeting. He agrees.

Carol is on the phone, trying to argue Mike into letting Frank come to the meeting. Frank smiles to himself to hear Mike has reservations about letting him. Finally, Mike agrees to Frank's coming.

Frank and Carol are talking to a young black woman who just came from Jamaica. They are in the basement of an upper-class home. About 20 people, old people, successful businessmen and army officers and their wives, and all-American kids are in the prayer circle. The intensity rises and is manifested in the same way as the first prayer meeting. An old man kisses Frank and talks to him in holy gibberish. The black woman prays simply to Jesus about Frank, which moves Frank. Mike comes into the room and stops the flow. He says God orders Frank to get up and walk, and if Frank doesn't have enough faith to try, Carol should have nothing more to do with him. Frank throws himself up out of his chair and falls flat on his face. Making no effort to break his fall, Mike and Carol pick him up and hug him. Mike tells him that he has proven himself.

Mike is asking for Frank's forgiveness for Mike's mistrust of him as they ride in the car.

We see Frank and Carol, both nude, rocking on the mattress in the bedroom. But when Frank starts trying to go into sexual feelings, she goes to her own bed. Frank just lies there, sad.

Carol is fixing breakfast for Frank. Frank decides to take the risk and asks her to make love to him. She says she can't until he is healed because his body turns her off sexually. She says she never has thought sexually about him. She says maybe they could get married after he is healed, but she isn't sure because she wants to be married to Jesus. They are interrupted by a phone call from Mike. Mike urges her to have nothing more to do with Frank, to forget about her promise to him and not to repay his money. She argues with him but won't hang up on him as Frank demands. Frank explodes, saying she has no right to keep him here without money or a way back, saying if she gets a plane ticket and gets him aboard, she can forget all her promises and hide from the world.

They are walking beside the river. He is telling her that he isn't mad; that she accidentally showed him what he has to do with his life, now he has to find a way to do it. They pass a dead dog and Frank's broken pointer.

We see Carol in the airport asking people to travel with Frank. A man agrees.

We see inside of the airplane. Carol is shaking Frank's hand and then walking way.

The film ends with a long take of a close up of Frank's sad face. He starts to cry, stops and breaks into a smile.

ABOUT FRANK MOORE

Frank Moore was an American performance artist, shaman, teacher, poet, essayist, painter, musician, and internet/television personality who experimented in art, performance, ritual, and shamanistic teaching from the late 1960s until his death in 2013 in Berkeley, California.

Moore is perhaps most well known as one of the NEA-funded artists targeted by Jesse Helms and the GAO (General Accounting Office) in the early 1990s for doing art that was labeled "obscene". Frank Moore was featured in the 1988 cult film Mondo New York, which chronicled the leading performance artists of that period. He is well known for long (5–48 hours) ritualistic performances with audience participation, nudity, and eroticism. But he has also become well known for his influential writings on performance, art, life, and cultural subversion, for his historic influence on the San Francisco Bay Area music and performance scene, and more recently for his online performance/video archive that has been viewed by over 32 million people worldwide.

Moore coined the word, "eroplay" to describe physical play between adults released from the linear goals of sex and orgasm. He explored this, and similar concepts in performance and ritual as a way for people to connect on a deep human level with each other beyond the social and cultural expectations and limitations, and as a way to melt isolation between people.

Moore has been an underground counter-culture hero and artistic inspiration for decades. He was born with cerebral palsy, could not walk or talk, and wrote books, directed plays, directed, acted in and edited films, regularly gave poetry readings, played piano, sang in ensemble music jams, and continued to lead bands in hard core punk clubs up and down the west coast until his death. He also produced a large collection of original oil and digital paintings that

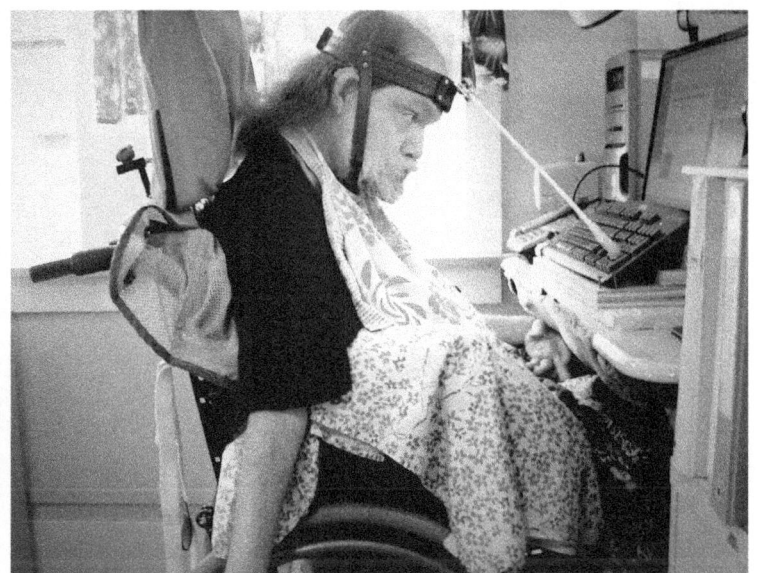
Frank Moore at the computer in his Berkeley home, 2012.

have been shown across the United States and in Canada. Moore communicated using a laser-pointer and a board of letters, numbers, and commonly used words.

Performance artist Annie Sprinkle considers Moore one of her teachers, and Moore performed with a host of performance and punk figures of the underground since the 1970s like Barbara Smith, Linda Sibio, The Feederz, and Dirk Dirksen - The Pope of Punk.

Frank Moore first came to be known in the 1970s as the creator of the popular cabaret show, *The Outrageous Beauty Revue*. In the 1980s he became one of the United States' foremost performance artists. In 1992 he was voted Best Performance Artist by the *San Francisco Bay Guardian*.

In the early 1990s he was targeted by Senator Jesse Helms.

From 1991 to 1999 Frank Moore published and edited the acclaimed underground zine, *The Cherotic (r)Evolutionary*.

In addition to his books, *Cherotic Magic*, *Art of a Shaman*, *Chapped Lap*, *Skin Passion* and numerous other self-published pieces, Frank Moore was widely published in various art and other periodicals. In artist Pamela Kay Walker's book, *Moving Over the Edge*, Moore is one of the artists featured as having "greatly impacted me and many people through their artistic expression and their lives."

Frank Moore's award-winning video works have shown throughout the U.S. and Canada, and in 2001 Moore began producing shows for Berkeley's public access channel, Berkeley Community Media, Channel 28. His shows continue to play several times each week.

In 2011, Frank launched his online performance and video retrospective on Vimeo. At the same time, he created the EROART group featuring videos by eroart artists from all over the world.

Frank Moore's Web of All Possibilities, www.eroplay.com, features a growing archive of his audio, video, visual and written work, as well as the work of other artists. He founded Love Underground Visionary Revolution (LUVeR) in 1999, a webstation combining live streaming and on-demand libraries of audio and video programming, described by Moore as a "non-corporate, d.i.y., totally uncensored, noncommercial, nonprofit internet-only communal collective with 24-hour 'live' programming (by amazing people) with 'no-limits' content." LUVeR ran until 2012.

In 2006, Moore announced his candidacy for the 2008 election for President of the United States. He became a qualified write-in candidate in 25 states. His campaign was responsible for reforming the write-in candidate qualifications and procedures in many states. His platform videos are available on YouTube.

Moore also hosted his regular internet show, "Frank Moore's Shaman's Den". Moore described it as a show that "will arouse, inspire, move, threaten you, not with sound bites, but with a two-hour (usually longer) feast of live streaming video. You might get an in-studio concert of bands from around the world … or poetry reading … or an in-depth conversation about politics, art, music, and LIFE with extremely dangerous people! But then you may see beautiful women naked dancing erotically. You never know, because you are in The Shaman's Den with Frank Moore." Video and audio archives of all of these Shaman's Den shows are available online.

Frank Moore performed regularly in the San Francisco Bay Area up until his death. His life and art are now being documented in a web video series called *Let Me Be Frank*.

As of September 2017, Frank Moore's work is now being archived at the Bancroft Library at the University of California, Berkeley. The collection is titled: "Frank Moore papers, approximately 1970-2013."

In April 2018, the Berkeley Art Museum and Pacific Film Archive (BAMPFA) accepted two of Frank's oil paintings into their permanent collection: *Mariah* (1977), and *Patti Smith* (1979). *Patti Smith* was also included in the BAMPFA exhibition, "Way Bay 2", in June of 2018.

In 2019, a collection of Frank Moore's work was archived at the Performistanbul Live Art Research Space in Istanbul, Turkey.

In 2023, a solo exhibit of Frank Moore's oil paintings, *Frank Moore / MATRIX 280: Theater of Human Melting* was held at BAMPFA, University of California, Berkeley Art Museum & Pacific Film Archive, 2155 Center Street Berkeley, CA.

In 2024, three of Frank's oil paintings, *Superman*, *Frankenstein*, and *Unicorn*, were part of the exhibition, *For Dear Life: Art, Medicine, and Disability*, at the Museum of Contemporary Art San Diego in La Jolla, California.

FRANK MOORE ONLINE

Frank Moore's Web Of All Possibilities
https://www.eroplay.com

The Shaman's Cave: performance archives, writings, articles, videos and more
https://www.eroplay.com/Cave/shaman.html

Books by Frank Moore
https://www.eroplay.com/books

Let Me Be Frank - web video series
https://frankadelic.com

Frank Moore Video Collection on The Internet Archive
https://archive.org/details/frank-moore-archives

Frank Moore Audio Archives on The Internet Archive
https://archive.org/details/FrankMoore

Frank Moore's Shaman's Den Archives: includes an archive of this online show
https://www.eroplay.com/underground/shamansden.html

Frank Moore Paintings
https://frankmoorepaintings.com/

Frank Moore Archives Blog
http://eroplay.org/

Frankly Speaking - featuring Frank Moore's writings
https://frankmoore.substack.com/

Frank Moore Digital Archives
https://archive-it.org/organizations/2683

Frank Moore on Wikipedia
https://en.wikipedia.org/wiki/Frank_Moore_(performance_artist)

www.ingramcontent.com/pod-product-compliance
Lightning Source LLC
Chambersburg PA
CBHW022110090426
42743CB00008B/788